I Am Not An
Anachronism

Gaining value at every career stage.

Don Polley

Published by: Don Polley and Associates
Trenton, Tennessee

I Am Not An Anachronism
Copyright © 2016 Don Polley

ISBN: 978-0692822418

Editor: Mary Reed
Cover: Kevin Adelsberger
Layout: Kevin Adelsberger
Headshot: Kevin Adelsberger

Contents

Chapter 1- Auspicious Beginnings — 1
Chapter 2- Blank Pages — 7
Chapter 3- Defining a Generation — 18
Chapter 4- Relocation Allocation — 24
Chapter 5- Nothing But Net.... — 30
Chapter 6- The Seeds That We Let Grow — 36
Chapter 7- All the Kings Horses and All the Kings Men... — 42
Chapter 8- Crawling from the Wreckage — 48
Chapter 9- Earning Recognition — 55
Chapter 10- The Jaded Edge — 61
Chapter 11- Now You See What You Missed — 68
Chapter 12- Two Scoops — 74
Chapter 13- Connecting the Dots — 82
Chapter 14- The End of the Beginning — 92
Chapter 15- Reconnecting — 99
Chapter 16- Rude Awakening — 108
Chapter 17- No Risk-No Reward — 116

Preface

Over the years, my friends and associates have told me many times that I should write a book. Like most folks, I simply brushed such an idea aside and moved on with my life. It did occur to me, though, that since I am able to add some flair and color to any story about my past experiences, that perhaps some day this would be a good idea. One of the most challenging things to me in writing a book is processing how to distill the information that you want to convey to the reader. I hope I have met that challenge in recounting my own workplace and life experiences from the mid-70s to today.

I began this undertaking in October 2015 with the intention of being completely done with it by April 2016. That was my plan. Ironically, I had mentioned in various management meetings over the years that "No plan survives contact with action." I should have known that now that I was in business for myself, this valuable lesson would apply to me as well. Experience, the wellspring of knowledge we have accrued, enables us to make good decisions in the future. I am pleased that my editor encouraged me to rewrite the preface to my book. I can now apply what I have discovered in my research over the past year to encourage both Millennials and Boomers to read and find merit in my endeavors.

When choosing a title for my book, I polled more than 150 millennials to see what they thought about my title so as to tweak their interest. Surprisingly, it was a great title selection to them as they had to Google it in order to see what it meant. It then tweaked their curiosity to find out what the book was about. Most of those polled were in college or college grads, which encouraged me to believe that I was on the right track. Since I began this project, I have spoken with a multitude of millennials at differing stages in their work and school careers to gain their point of view regarding our society and the challenges they had to face to succeed.

As I looked back upon the evolution of my own life and a career that spans more than four decades, I found that I could relate to Millennial characteristics in many ways. Though I am rooted in a generation in which it is not uncommon to be a part of one company for much of one's career, I have had more than 25 different jobs. Entrepreneurs understand the value of dedication and loyalty and its impact upon their business ventures. Surrounded by such influence over the years, I found it either odd or impractical that I did not fit into the standard mold.

From kindergarten through college, I went to 14 different schools. In almost every case, I fit into the exception rather the norm. I found myself being the new kid having to adapt to a different culture in order to fit in. I became outgoing and very attentive to my surroundings to be able to grasp the positive elements of my situation. I chose to craft my own unique identity so as not to be ordinary but extra-ordinary – and this proved to be a challenge most of the time. Oftentimes in life, the paths we choose lead to much different destinations as time becomes a variable instead of a standard.

I began to learn very early in life that continuous learning would be necessary in order to be able to stay ahead of the curve. For example, the business degree I pursued in the 1970s would not be earned until 2004 during a layoff period from Goodyear (where I first tried to get a job in 1976).

Preface

When I first graduated from a community college in 1983, I had dreams of attending a four-year university to see how far my educational background would take me as I moved forward in my career. Family concerns have a huge influence upon how limited resources are dispersed, and sometimes dreams have to be put on hold. Looking to leverage my degree for what it was to be worth, I became dissatisfied with being a laborer in the Magic Chef plant where I worked while going to school. The decision to leave a job that had both stability and tenure would lead me back into a leadership role in business once again. In order to achieve success, I had to move first to Missouri and then to Tennessee. I can relate to the restless spirit of Millennials as they seek opportunities to turn their academic success into an aspiring career in their chosen field.

Empathy, honesty and humility, which are the key elements of my leadership style, are the basis of servant leadership. The strengths that served me so well in the 20th century were still in demand in the 21st-century workplace. Today they are referred to as soft skills and instrumental in dealing with the needs of employees.

In the past, I was derided for my exceptional people skills in order to motivate others in business. Now I seek to highlight those skills as being a benchmark for my business as a consultant. The Don Polley experience relates positively to both segments of the generational workplace. Millennials are eager to learn what it takes in order to succeed in business, and most companies are heavily vested in trying to find out what it takes to attract, engage and retain the best talent.

I have always maintained a different outlook in order to gauge my current situation. This process has enabled me to be able to distill what is necessary in order to successfully move forward into the digital age.

    My goal with my new career as a generational workplace consultant is to build a bridge of understanding between Millennials (age 35 and younger) and Boomers (age 36 and above). I have witnessed and personally experienced many of the challenges facing Millennials today. I can relate to the potential conflicts that can arise in trying to communicate specifics from one generation to the other. Essentially we need to celebrate our similarities and respect our differences. Elements from both sides of the generational spectrum are vitally important to defining our present as well as clearing a pathway for future prosperity and success.

    Though I am of the Boomer generation and many, many of my life's experiences are of the Millennial generation, I am not an anachronism. Instead, I am uniquely placed in a position to help today's managers relate to the growing numbers of talented Millennials they find in their workplace. I am not an anachronism. This is my time.

Chapter 1
Auspicious Beginnings

I Am Not An **Anachronism** | Don Polley

An old adage suggests that we all have 20/20 hindsight. As I sit here at my laptop on a blustery Saturday afternoon in October, I find myself waxing somewhat nostalgic. I suppose one might say that I am having '70s flashbacks without the amenities provided by chemical enhancements. I am writing a book about my life, my career and my subsequent evolution as a Baby Boomer entering the workplace in the mid 1970s to the fast-paced, technology-based workplace of the 21st Century.

I recently wrote a review posted on Amazon.com for a book on time management, and it inspired me to pursue something I have had on the back burner for a long time – writing a book. It is going to be somewhat autobiographical in nature and classified as nonfiction, so as to reflect or depict the era in which I lived, came of age and thrived in the decades that followed.

Early on, I was an entrepreneur of sorts. We were living in a metropolitan area, and I would borrow my mother's fold-down shopping cart and walk around alleys, vacant lots, and anywhere that people would discard their Coke bottles. I received a deposit on them if I returned them to a store that sold the products.

I used the money to purchase comic books, which provided me with entertainment; our TV was a 13-inch, black-and-white portable on a makeshift television stand. My mother gladly purchased a Webster's dictionary for me so I could look up the words from the dialogue between the

Auspicious Beginnings

superhero and supervillain. My supply chain of Coke bottles was interrupted when my family moved to a small town in Southern Illinois.

After beginning my education in Chicago, I transferred after two years to a school in that small town and lived with my grandparents. The town had two elementary schools, and I attended both of them. Then my mother remarried and moved me back to Chicago where I attended a new public school.

The one common thread between the urban and rural school was that, before class, we stood up with a hand over our heart and said the "Pledge of Allegiance." During the following year, due to social unrest and problems in Chicago's public schools, I enrolled in a Catholic school across the street from the dry cleaners that my mother operated.

As it turned out, I was the only non-Catholic student in the entire school. I can only speculate on what the cost of admission was at that time. Sadly, from this time forward, the "Pledge of Allegiance" was no longer practiced in school. I can no longer use it as a common thread as I continued to have changes in my lifestyle, academics and overall socio-economic environments as I bounced between urban and rural America in the Midwest. Still trying to shield me from social and economic unrest, my family moved from Chicago to Evansville, Indiana, where I was to attend seventh grade. I didn't stay long, though. By mid-year we were moving again as my parents sought jobs with higher pay and more opportunity. I moved to Carmi, Illinois, to stay with family while my parents went back to Chicago. Once again, as January rolled around, I was the new kid in school again.

      I would finish my elementary school academic career graduating the eighth grade in Chicago. Then, I enrolled in an all-male high school with prestigious programs because I scored well on an aptitude test. During orientation, my high school curriculum was laid out in front of me. I was told I would be enrolled in ROTC (Reserved Officer Training Corps), as my test results indicated that I possessed the potential to be a strong leader. ROTC would have led to a career in the military. Just to be clear, this was in 1971, and the Vietnam War was in full swing. I wasn't so sure about going to this school and being in ROTC.

      Suddenly, the conversations I had with protesters in "Old Town" in Chicago had a new meaning for me. As I read the leaflets passed out by long-haired, trench-coat-wearing "hippies," who all looked like either singer/songwriter Bob Dylan or actor Tommy Chong, the subject matter seemed to gain my interest. It was at that point in my life that my mother's only son wanted to explore a different academic path than the bright future offered by the technical academy I was about to attend. Wouldn't you know it, the path to my future led once again to Southern Illinois, to the small town where I was born.

      Before I attended my first day of class in the new high school with its ROTC program, I transferred to a high school in Carmi, Illinois. Leadership and change, change and leadership – even at that stage in my life there seemed to be a correlation. To be fair, I did have the great privilege of attending all four years in the high school in Carmi.

Auspicious Beginnings

As I entered as a freshman, the high school had just combined the smaller high schools in the area into a township high school. For the first time in a while, I was not the only new kid in school. This enabled me to form friendships with students who had been disenfranchised from their home schools, and we formed bonds that in some cases would last a lifetime. I learned how to earn trust and build lasting relationships. This ability would serve me well as I moved forward in my professional career.

In my early high school years, I also took classes in typing and Latin. Because I was not designated to become a secretary after graduation, I had to learn how to type on a Royal typewriter that had a manual return. The limited number of electric typewriters we had available went to those on the secretarial path. But I did learn the home keys and how to type well enough without mistakes to earn a good grade in the class. Once again, that capability has served me well even to this day.

I make note of my enrollment in Latin as a foreign language primarily to show the impact it made on my academic endeavors as I pursued options for post-secondary education after graduation. It is amazing how many words in the English language come from Latin derivatives. This was another useful element I integrated into my skillset before pursuing a career.

I was raised in a time where faith in God, country and the American Way was instilled in our minds by our families, peers and the media – even as it experienced growth and change. The pursuit of the American Dream was a real goal and aspiration for anyone, no matter his or her walk of life. This has been the one common denominator for me in a life buffeted by continual change and uncertain future. I learned to adapt, recalibrate and pursue the most expedient path in which to prosper and grow.

As I researched the differences presented by each generation to substantiate the premise of this writing, I learned the formative years are from 5 through 18. This is what led me to title my book, "I Am Not an Anachronism."

As I continued my research, I found that my ability to overcome the challenges I faced and achieve the level of success I enjoyed over the years was a by-product of the mindset I developed during the course of my life. It occurred to me that my years of struggle were not a handicap but an asset; I had gained tacit knowledge, wisdom and experience. Though the window of opportunity is not very wide, this is my time to share what I learned about generational diversity and how to create a harmonic balance across the generational divide.

Chapter 2
Blank Pages

I Am Not An **Anachronism** | Don Polley

Our saga begins in 1974 in a small rural town in Southern Illinois. My first "paying job" beyond working with a family member involved working for a semi-retired gentleman who operated a printing service out of his shed behind his house. I responded to an ad in the local newspaper and was asked if I could type, follow instructions and knew how to spell and use a dictionary.

I was told that there was a right way to do things, a wrong way to do things, and his way of doing things, which was the only way I was to concern myself with. I was to learn that he was not the only one to practice such an orientation to the tasks I had been hired to accomplish. To his satisfaction, I was a quick study and earned my dollar-an-hour wage, which was the minimum at that time. He taught me to show up on time and pay attention to detail, and he encouraged me to develop a work ethic that would apply to any job I would ever encounter for the rest of my life. He taught me that anything worth doing was worth doing right the first time you did it. Mistakes were not tolerated during my tenure in his employ.

I learned all that for a dollar an hour. I began to realize the value of having a mentor, and from that time forward, I knew we could add value to anything we do if we apply ourselves to the task. This was the beginning of a career path that would zig and zag across decades as well as generational divides.

When I began my career, the workplace had only two generations – the Traditionalists and my generation, which would come to be known as the "Baby Boomers." Traditionalists were firm believers in on-the-job training, quality, serving the customer, high productivity and efficiency. This was a great place for us to start, but they had no idea of the amazing potential they had unleashed once they let us go on our own. The Baby Boomers revolutionized the workplace, culture and society, and they took productivity to unprecedented levels through innovation and automation with a capacity to continually learn and evolve. Information was power, and we wanted it all. The ideology of "that is the way it has always been done," was transformed into "why can we not do it this way?"

The guidance counselor at my high school believed that because my parents were not pillars of the community, and I was not involved with sports, I should set the bar low in aspirations and endeavor to achieve some modicum of success in my life. This was his determination despite the better-than-average scores I obtained on my ACT and SAT standardized tests. Everyone in my family was honest and hardworking, but at that point only one had obtained a college degree. This was an indication of my supposed lot in life as perceived by those who were educated to intelligently make such a determination. Having moved to Southern Illinois from Chicago, I was not very impressed by the assessment of a somewhat biased administrator in a small rural town. Because I would not be compelled to actively participate in the Vietnam War, I began to speculate upon a different direction for my life.

I got a job with a discount retail chain that had a multitude of stores across different states. The printer was pleased with the progress I had made, and I thanked him for his part in my career path.

I encountered my next significant career challenge while I was still 15 years old. I was hired to work in a discount retail box store in town though I was not supposed to be eligible for hire until I was 16. I looked and conducted myself maturely, and because my birthday was late in the year and the manager was moving to another store, he put my paperwork through.

The new manager was from Red Wing, Minnesota, and he was in culture shock when I actually did turn 16 and he realized the oversight.

By that time, he was relying on my organizational skills, knowledge of the community, and capacity to work well with those who were much older than I was. He was also impressed with my commitment to customer service. I was able to focus on staff and the customer base so he could concentrate on improving our position within our district. He was young, bold, innovative and driven to make our store a stepping stone in his career path within the company. I was young, energetic and open to learning everything he could teach me about the business. In my mind, I was defining my career path.

Each quarter our store made radical improvements in sales over the previous year, and we were also moving up by volume to surpass stores in our district that were larger and in a better market. This drew the attention of our district manager. My manager's acknowledgement of my efforts to achieve the goals led to my promotion to assistant manager, even though I was not 18 yet. Unable to curb my enthusiasm for good fortune, I would soon learn that this would turn out to be a mixed blessing for me and my career.

During the summer of my 17th year, I would graduate high school, help to set up grand openings for new stores for the parent company, part ways with my mentor and friend from Minnesota, and learn how to deal with a new manager who regarded my youth as something to be leveraged. I learned an invaluable lesson that summer and into the fall of 1975: Age can be a liability, but value trumps liability every time.

Unfortunately, I was only able to apply what I had learned on a limited basis at that juncture in my career. I had learned how to offset the stigma of my youth by inspiring folks of all ages to work together to achieve a specific goal. Even at that early age in my life, I had learned how to blend generational differences in a way that produced a positive outcome for all parties involved.

For the graduating class of 1975, the options available in our area were somewhat limited – college, moving away, working in the oil fields or trying to get in one of the local coal mines. Despite the fact that President Nixon had abolished the draft and ended the Vietnam War, I still had fellow graduates and friends join the peacetime military.

I was convinced that I was not an anachronism, because I missed the war and positioned myself to pursue a challenging and rewarding career in retail.

The events that followed taught me about supply and demand, real-life economics, and what happens when you are young, inexperienced and pressed into playing corporate politics for a seat at the table with the "grownups." I soon found out that hard work and positive results paled in comparison to cronyism and manipulation, which could change the way one's efforts were perceived by those who did not have direct contact with the situation.

I am not upset at the way the chain of events played out, but I do wish the timing had been a little different. I was called upon to assist in setting up new stores for the parent company, and I did well enough to receive notice throughout the company. This led to a potential opportunity for advancement and a springboard to a rewarding career with the parent company. Just as my mentor from Red Wing had indicated, I was farther along on my career path than others in my generation.

During one of the break periods over the summer in my home store, another significant discount retail chain – Walmart – contacted me with a job offer. I respectfully turned it down because the company I was with was sound, progressive and growing. I didn't know much about Walmart at the time. Information was not as widely shared in those days or as accessible as it is today. Had I been more familiar with the value of stock options and the power of investments, I would have undoubtedly made a different choice.

I was overcome by the impatience of youth because I had to be at least 18 before I could be promoted to a larger store, and I found it to be unbearable to work for a new manager who took advantage of every opportunity to get out of the store and not return until the next day. Once I discovered that he delayed my promotion so I could help him transition to the new area, my aspiring career in retail ended somewhat unceremoniously.

Instead of being patient and considering the liability of my age, I did the most mature thing I could think of and went to work in the oil field. This experience taught me that value trumps liability every time. Had I been a little more patient, as well as more receptive to those who were older but had my best interests in mind, things may have worked out differently for me.

Graduating high school at 17 is hard enough, but

having to make adult decisions before you are 18 is, well, challenging at best. Working seven days a week outside during winter in Southern Illinois has a tendency to make one appreciate air conditioning in the summer and heat in the winter. The winters seemed colder in those days. I learned how fresh air could feel when the temperature was plummeting by the hour, and your job required you to work outside. I was on morning tower, which was from 10 p.m. to 6 a.m. and generally the coldest part of the day.

The money was good, however, and overtime was always readily available. The primary way to get a day off was to get someone from another crew to pull a double shift for you. I did it a few times and decided that more money was okay, but I did not have any time to enjoy the fruits of my labor.

A job working on an oil rig paid well, but working seven days a week got old to an 18-year-old young man who had envisioned his career moving in a somewhat different direction.

After I tried the oil field gig, I felt it was time to move from the town where I graduated to Union City in West Tennessee. I had family I could stay with, and I also had some friends who worked at the local tire plant, Goodyear. They seemed fairly certain they could get me on board in a big company with a bright future. I once again set my sights on steady employment, opportunities for advancement and job security by working for Goodyear, a Fortune 500 company. It was 1976 – and I did not succeed. However, this particular plant would have a role later in my career.

Keep in mind, I was only 19 years old, and life still had many lessons in store for me. At this point, after trying the oil field and moving away, the next logical step to me was to go to school. But with my limited resources, I needed to work to offset the cost of tuition and books, as well as fund my living expenses.

I found a job at another molded rubber plant in Carmi where I graduated high school. I thought that was ironic because I moved out of state to get a job in a rubber plant. I was placed on third shift so I could go to school during the day and work at night. I made accommodations for everything except sleeping and found myself battling fatigue from time to time.

I learned about compounds, mixing, and nuances that were involved in expediting rubber gaskets primarily for the automotive industry. I ended up spending the next two and a half years at the rubber plant, learning valuable knowledge and gaining skills that would benefit me decades later when I actually did get a job at Goodyear in West Tennessee.

I also had an opportunity to perform in the capacity of a third-shift supervisor, which enabled me to gain insights as to why employees desire the third shift and why management designates certain employees to begin their tenure with the company in that capacity. My staff ranged in age from 18 to 53. Being on the younger end of that spectrum, I found myself able to build relationships and gain trust from my entire crew because of my previous experience with generational diversity in the retail setting.

During my tenure, our third-shift crew out-produced the other crews with the lowest scrap rate. We also earned high marks on attendance and productivity. It was at this point in my professional career in leadership that I realized that the perception of age as a liability was a myth to be dispelled, as value trumps liability every time.

You could pursue your goals and dreams, even in the mid 1970s, without cell phones, Internet access and GPS. It was easy because none of those things had been invented. We did have eight-track tape players and CB radios in our vehicles, and you just couldn't beat the nightly news to keep track of what was going on in the world.

Initially, my generation was labeled as useless and listless with no ambition, no drive and an uncertain future. It was a reasonable estimation because our decade fell between the rebellion and social unrest of the 1960s and the 1980s with the Iran Contra affair and the savings and loan crisis in the economy. Also, the greatest nation in the world elected Ronald Reagan, a former Hollywood actor, as President and while the world was beset with turmoil.

This was to be the melting pot and the foundation of the generation that would come to be known as Baby Boomers. We were forced to deal with high interest rates, inflation, layoffs, downsizing and corporate greed as a byproduct of "trickle-down economics." The Supreme Court decision of Roe vs. Wade also set the stage to ignite a wave of women's liberation across the country.

At the beginning of the 1980s, I got a job at an appliance plant, Magic Chef, in Southern Illinois. It had just made the transition from one brand name to another. I relate to indicate to younger readers that change is not something that was created in the 21st century. Those of us perceived as old and unable to adapt to change have actually been exposed to change and the challenges it brings all of our lives.

My first experience with labor unions came from a warehouse in Southern Illinois where workers were repre-

I Am Not An **Anachronism** | Don Polley

sented by the AFL-CIO. I was working there when Magic Chef called me to interview for a job position. At the warehouse job, I was forced or "strongly coerced" into working 12-hour shifts each night. I was on second shift. If you were new and not yet in the union, you had no choice but to work overtime. On nearly every occasion, I agreed to work overtime. On my 29th day of working at the warehouse, I was once again asked to work overtime. This time I told them I couldn't do it. I had a 7 a.m. job interview at Magic Chef. The warehouse informed me that there was no need for me to report to work that evening. It would have been my 30th day at the warehouse, which is when I was eligible to join the union. The appliance plant offered a significant drop in salary, but I felt I made the right choice, and I worked there for the next five years.

During my tenure at Magic Chef, I had the opportunity to shake the hand of a man who would become President of the United States during a campaign stop. I respectfully declined because I did not agree with his politics. I also had the opportunity to go back to school at a local community college to obtain an associate degree in science, which was no easy task while working full time. My first experience with computers was in a college class where we learned to work with floppy discs, MS-DOS and LOTUS. You had to write your own programs. Not only was the preparation of a program cumbersome, you needed a noisy ball printer with two-tone large perforated paper to print it. I had no idea at the time what a "laptop" computer was, but I had a friend who took his Apple computer to work each day because his company had no budget for technology. Needless to say, he and his "Mac" made an impression upon upper management, and they gave him the resources he required to function in his position.

Young people today do not realize the hurdles we had to overcome in order to achieve the success that we accomplished as a generation. We believed in hard work, dedication and the pursuit of the American dream. The war was finally over in Vietnam. We had a president in office who was a man of good character and a strong leader, and as a nation, we were finally inspired once again to pursue health, happiness and the American way.

Despite this optimism, my generation had to address double-digit inflation and a prime interest rate that would soar as high as 21.5 percent in June 1982. Between this and the savings and loan crisis and the challenges presented by the financial industry crisis, we found our dire situation to be a rite of passage into the 1980s.

Chapter 3
Defining a Generation

Once again, impediments prevented me from improving my status in the appliance manufacturing plant that subsidized my livelihood over the past five years. At this point in my life, the number of Baby Boomers in the workforce was putting a greater emphasis on education and impacted the way business was done in the eighties.

By the end of the decade, the number of Boomers in the workplace would eclipse Traditionalists. If that was not enough to deal with, along with the women's liberation movement, the offspring of Boomers – Generation X – was entering the workforce.

Those of the Traditional generation learned to come to grips with gradual change. They prospered by nurturing and then unleashing Baby Boomers into the landscape of business and how things were to be done. To satisfy our inherent desire to obtain our "rightful share" of the pie, as well as pave the path to prosperity for our children, we were driven to continually question, improvise and improve upon anything that translated into our definition of the path to success.

Our need to better communicate led to the creation of car phones, cordless telephones, fax machines, and of course, computer technology. Not only was our work life evolving, our home lives were changing as electronic devices became smaller, faster and capable of more and more memory. The era of the Baby Boomer was now in full swing as we desired, wanted and pursued more and more.

We were too busy to realize that our children were paying attention to what was going on around them, and we continually substituted television and other things to keep them entertained and distracted. This overall disconnect led to the popularity of Nintendo and other games that could be plugged into any TV, and it replaced trips to the bowling alley or video arcade.

They wondered why they had to visit with grandparents to get the down-to-earth, common-sense knowledge and information that was so readily available to us as we grew up. They wanted to know what challenges they would face as they approached their time to make an impact in the world. We seemed to provide them with everything they desired except quality time with us. This led to the overriding sense of entitlement that caused Boomers so much grief as we tried to mentor them into the workplace and society, just as the Traditionalists had done with us.

I began to realize that the underlying elements of my success were based on what I had learned in a leadership role in my youth. This experience combined with my diverse academic background and my personal experiences with all three generations that were at play in driving the gross national product at that time. We had Reagan as our president, high interest rates, trickle-down economics and what would appear to be economic prosperity. We had a peacetime army, and opportunity seemed to be everywhere just for the taking. Needless to say, the American dream was alive and well. Not only was my generation impatient to obtain success, we were impatient in getting what we wanted, when we wanted it. Despite the financial wisdom that was passed along to us to be austere and save for the future, we embraced debt, not understanding that it would create an almost insurmountable impediment to our success as we moved forward in our lives.

It was during this time that I decided to go back to school and obtain an associate degree so I could finish what I started. Though I had attended Southern Illinois Community College, I didn't get enough credits to graduate with the associates degree in business administration I was seeking. I enrolled in John A. Logan Community College, this time seeking an associates degree in life sciences.

Once I graduated from John A. Logan in 1983, I reflected on my overall career path up to that point. I contemplated pursuing a bachelor's degree at a nearby university, but I became restless because I worked hard to achieve academic success. My initial experience with academics after high school did not culminate with graduation for a variety of reasons. So this diploma gave me a particular degree of personal satisfaction, and I was anxious to put it to work.

I succeeded in my objective of getting a degree, but I also met the mother of my daughter at that time, which impacted the way I would use my limited financial resources.

No longer satisfied with working in a factory like Magic Chef, I was determined to leverage my education, experience, diverse background and leadership capability into a successful professional career. With a very brief stint in the insurance business, I found myself engaged in procuring advertising for a quarterly publication and became familiar with the various elements involved with running a business. This was an opportunity for me to utilize all my underused drivers for success. Telemarketing was a large part of the medium used to reach out to potential customers to solicit their business. In other words, communication was the key to achieving objectives and triggering bonuses and other incentives to perpetuate the business. My skills as a coach and trainer led to bonuses and an attractive salary to go along with my commission.

This opportunity also led me to St. Louis where my

urban background enabled me to acclimate to a metropolitan area quickly and seamlessly. Unfortunately, the late nights at the office, weekend golf games and occasional business trips were not endearing qualities to my family, and I was strongly urged to find a different means by which to earn a living. As such, I passed on what could have been the opportunity of my lifetime – getting in on the ground floor of a local company that was going to produce bottled water. The owners were convinced I could be an integral part of their startup. They were impressed with my leadership skills, sales acumen and enthusiasm. Once again, if I had access to the technology that is so plentifully available today, my decision may have been entirely different.

In deference to my wife's desire for stability and benefits, I accepted a position in a job shop in St. Louis County working with blueprints and low tolerances. Once again, the career experiences from my past would lead to a smooth transition. The ownership was immediately enamored with my attitude and the way in which I worked with others despite being the new kid on the block.

With ingenuity and innovation, I instituted procedures that enabled them to turn around some repeat jobs in less than half the time. My skills working with people across cultural and generational divides helped me to become a productive element of the team quickly and effectively.

My new entry-level salary was much smaller than what I made running the advertising agency. I managed to fill that void by accepting a part-time position in sales at an auto brokerage not far from where I worked. Once again, my people skills served me well, and I soon began earning more than $500 per week for working only 12 hours a week. Life was good, and everything seemed to be moving in the right direction. When we engulf ourselves in providing for the financial needs of our family, we can easily be drawn away by the things that are really important in our lives.

Chapter 4
Relocation Allocation

Relocation Allocation

We see things in the news all the time in large metropolitan areas that cause us to feel empathy for those who have suffered due to loss, tragedy or senseless crime. For most of us, we really don't identify with something until it strikes close to home. A blatant act of violence at mid-day in a neighborhood very close to mine instilled a sense of fear in my spouse that could only be abated by moving away to a place where such atrocities are rare.

Immediate plans were put into place to move from the city to a more rural setting. Because I had family in West Tennessee, it seemed like a good compromise based on the gravity of the situation and its impact on my family's livelihood. Once again my avarice, which seemed to define my generation, would not permit me to easily part ways with the city in which I made my home. When I put in my notice to leave, my company made an extremely attractive offer to entice me to change my mind and stay in the city. My family had already moved to West Tennessee, so their actions only added to my trepidation. My spouse, however, was beyond reason or compromise for any alternative, no matter what the incentive. If only I could have had access to the Internet at that time or had a tablet or smart phone on which to research the facts before making my decision. Perhaps the direction of my life would have been different.

It does not require a psychologist to determine that this situation may have led to some marital disputes and disagreements over the next few months. Prospects for employment in West Tennessee were plentiful at the time, but compensation, compared to what I had been accustomed, was sorely lacking. The idea that companies moved South for cheaper labor hit much closer to home for me.

I Am Not An **Anachronism** | Don Polley

I had experience, education and drive to go along with the people skills I accrued over the years, which seemed to be an asset in every endeavor except my relationship to my spouse. She resigned to move to Southern Illinois where she had some family, and I was determined to make a go of it in West Tennessee. A decade that started with hope, promise, prospects and opportunity would end much the same. The career value I gained over the years came at a tremendous personal cost in the short haul, but it would prove to turn into amazing motivational capital as I moved forward professionally. I decided during my initial venture into Tennessee, that if opportunity presented itself, I would make the transition once again, but this time with conviction to stay put for the long haul.

Despite having limited job opportunities available, the value and skills I attained in advertising and using telemarketing would serve me well. I found myself working for a company that sold advertisement signs on benches. It was a fascinating concept to me at the time. I was astonished at the demand for such advertising in rural areas across several different states.

Being able to communicate with business owners from different generational backgrounds proved to be quite useful in keeping myself in good standing with the company. I worked well with everyone, from the bench maker to the delivery driver who needed to move product in order to make a living. It was certainly not a career-defining move, but it was a good place to start the first of what is now 28 years of living in Tennessee.

The next opportunity that presented itself was at Dresden Products, a fabrication facility that made drawer slides and cabinet hardware. I was familiar with little in that operation, but I was a fast learner and knew how to read complex blueprints and work with low tolerances. I fit in at once in the quality assurance department.

In a short time, I became adept in all phases of the manufacturing process. I could relate with my co-workers and build relationships based on trust and understanding. Once I became quality manager, I found that the only true ally I had in the facility among the management staff was the plant manager. He explained the parameters of expectations pertaining to my position and told me he was the only one I needed to answer to.

This enamored me to the production staff, but produced a somewhat tenuous relationship at times with my peers. I discovered that during slow periods, quality was vitally important. However, when production schedules increased dramatically during busy seasons, compromise and rationality needed to enter the equation in order to find maximum profitability without sacrificing customer satisfaction. The plant closed down. I learned a great many valuable lessons during my tenure at the company and tried to glean as much tacit knowledge from skilled professionals in other areas of the plant – all of which would serve me well later in my career.

Because I possessed such a varied background and creative skillset, I did not have much difficulty finding another job. In those days, opportunities were plentiful, and there always seemed to be a shortage of motivated individuals ready to take ownership and engage in the business at hand.

In those days, unlike today when a transient workforce seems to be the norm, a job history of a variety of places of employment was not perceived as a positive trait. Fortunately for me, value trumps any perceived liability every time. It did then, and I am convinced that is still the same in today's evaluation process. I was displaying characteristics of a Millennial, even at that stage in my career.

I discovered that my leadership style of empathy, honesty and humility would play well with those on the production floor as well as subordinates on my quality assurance team. I learned years earlier that respect had to be earned, and once trust was established, it was far easier to maintain than it was to obtain.

The experiences I accrued also enabled me to navigate my way successfully in the realm of company politics. I have always been a people's advocate, which inevitably created friction with those in upper management. I was still learning how to become adept at managing internal customer relations in a manner that would be acceptable to those that resided in the front office. During this period of time, it was not commonplace for upper management or senior staff to interact with those on the production floor.

At this point in my professional career, it was not my youth that was a hindrance to establishing cooperative relationships, but rather my contemporaries who seemed to create conflict. They were envious of my ability to understand and relate to all parties across the generational divide. I had even learned how to properly address women who had been heavily influenced by the liberation movement from my experiences in school and the workplace. When you learn to gain value from every career stage, it is a resource that you can use to further advance your career as you move forward.

Training and mentoring became second nature to me, and I incorporated them into how I performed my duties on a daily basis. As long as the senior staff felt they were in control of the situation, they were perfectly happy to allow you to proceed in accomplishing your tasks. The cooperative effort on the part of schedulers, production staff and my department led to the successful implementation of Just-In-Time, or JIT, ordering of raw materials. The program effectively built up bonuses and the bottom line, and it galvanized my position with the plant manager in a job that I wanted to blossom into other opportunities over time.

With companies flourishing around us and the economy moving in a positive direction, my company was sold to a local group, which quickly altered the culture of the business. Given the ultimatum of accepting the changes or moving on, I sought a different direction in my career. I found out later I made the right choice, as the company soon went out of business.

I began to realize that the culture of a company is just as important as any compensation package that may be offered, sometimes even more so. Undaunted by my decision to move forward, I soon found gainful employment in another production facility. But I knew from the outset that it was not going to be a career move for me.

I would like to point out that, during this time, the Career Center, which was formerly known as the Unemployment Office, was actually proactive in helping people find jobs. The center was staffed with dedicated and skilled professionals who treated people with dignity and respect during a point in their lives when a kind word and encouragement made a tremendous difference.

Chapter 5
Nothing But Net....

Although I had managed to stay continuously employed since my high school days in Southern Illinois, I found myself reflecting from time to time on what might have been. The contrasts to the young people of today are staggering. They have the opportunity to research a company or organization and find out things about its culture, benefits, and the potential to make an impact in any opening for which they may have interest. I had to hire on and make the most out of any opportunity that might present itself to me based upon my skills, background and experience.

I must confess that, occasionally, brute strength and awkwardness seemed to be the most expedient approach to overcoming a challenge or problematic situation. In those days I referred to my skill as problem-solving ability, but today it is referred to as critical thinking. Much like a basketball going into a rim, I was still seeking a place where I could fit in. Anytime I played basketball in high school, my favorite sound was the swish of the net as the ball sailed cleanly through it.

The next phase of my career led me to contract packaging. I managed to obtain a position as a corporate quality manager at a facility in Milan, Tennessee, a small town about 35 miles south of the parent plant in Dresden. The primary business in the main facility was packing book displays for retail outlets across the nation. (At that time, I had no idea I would write a book that could be displayed on the shelves of the same brick-and-mortar stores.)

Life has an amusing way of subjecting you to ironic twists as you move forward throughout the course of your career. This is just another nugget of the wisdom that I hope my younger readers will obtain from my humble offering on the evolution of a Baby Boomer. My new job featured chal-

I Am Not An **Anachronism** | Don Polley

lenge, an opportunity to learn and grow, and a platform to use everything I learned to date over the course of my career.

One of the first challenges I faced was dealing with generational diversity and its impact in the fast-paced, ever-changing, constantly-evolving world of contract packaging. In order to fill the new role, it was vitally important that I communicated quality standards and procedures in a manner that was understood and readily implemented throughout the organization. With the guidance and support of upper management, it was not an insurmountable task. The average age of the production staff was around 19, and turnover among that age group was problematic. When I gained the confidence and trust of the team leaders along the packaging lines, my job became easier.

My first order of business was to familiarize myself with the product and its process from supplier to packager to supplier. My main focus was satisfying the customer needs in book packaging, which was the bulk of our business. Upper management gave me a relative amount of autonomy, but I had to submit for approval any changes in metrics or guidelines that I instituted to expedite the process.

Everything was on a deadline. It was the nature of the business. The company had gained a reputation for rapid turnaround, but it was also known for an occasional lapse in the high quality of standards required by the customer. Initially, I was unfamiliar with the quality standards desired by the customer, but the customer's staff was more than happy to oblige in bringing me up to speed on what was expected.

I have always been customer centric in my approach to any business, and my grasp of working with those from differing generational backgrounds would once again serve me well. I made the transition from metal fabrication to books – just as those who hired me were confident I would do. Gain value at every career stage; you never know when it might open a door of opportunity for you later.

Contract packaging was a daily challenge that enabled me to refine skills I already possessed. I also gained experience with leadership, negotiation and managing the impact of generational diversity in the workplace. In order to gain empathy with the younger employees, who were predominant in the workforce at the time, it became necessary to understand their motivational factors. Wage and longevity were not key components to most of the young people on staff. However, doing a good job and being seen as a good co-worker seemed to rank high on their list of desired outcomes. Once they were onboard with what was expected, it became a simple matter of reinforcing the procedure and giving them some positive acknowledgement for a job well done.

I had already learned how to relate to the generation ahead of me, which was a benefit now. These were the deciders, for the most part, in the corporate mix, and without their blessings, it was difficult to get anything done. I earned the respect and trust of my contemporaries in my own generation as a man of integrity, honesty and conviction. Now, I had to apply empathy, honesty and humility as leadership tools in order to relate to and instruct the next generation.

Sincerity goes a long way with those who perceive you to be an advocate for their hopes, dreams and aspirations in the generational workplace. Though young, they acknowledge that they lack the experience and the expertise to broker an amicable solution to problems that arise from day to day. When you can establish yourself as a people's advocate in the role of a quality manager, most of the issues you address are from the top down and not the bottom up. Due to the fast-paced nature of the business, I adopted the rule of Three C's – coordination, cooperation and communication. It's easy to remember and implement once everyone is on board with the plan.

Having established a mutual understanding with the production floor, the next step was to clarify the customer's quality standards. My penchant for being customer centric, as well as being articulate, was helpful in gaining the trust of the in-house quality staff in Tennessee. The comics I read so voraciously as a youth familiarized me with many of the facets involved in publications.

To gain value at every career stage, it's important to pay attention, look around and listen, and learn from those eager to pass wisdom and knowledge that enable you to better serve their needs. I quickly formed a relationship of respect and trust with the quality staff in both of the book production plants we did business with at the time. Managing a generational workplace is a skill, and it is not easily accrued.

The ISBN number was the key to identify where and how the books were packaged for distribution. Our function was to unpack the books, identify the titles and ISBN numbers, build the displays, fill them with the appropriate books, and then label the packaged displays. Then we sent them back to the vendor for shipment and distribution across the nation. It was interesting, fast paced and ever changing, but that was just part of the business. I did not realize at the time that I was gaining value that would enable me to better and more completely understand the way in which business would be conducted 20 years later.

Once I gained a firm understanding of the book aspect

of the packaging business, I was introduced to an appliance manufacturer and its distribution warehouse about 35 miles away. Irony was at work in my career once again. It was Magic Chef, the appliance manufacturer I worked for in the late 1970s until 1984. But in this case, we were packaging product to be sent to the distribution warehouse in Milan – the same town as our subsidiary branch.

Fortunately, I had built a strong relationship with both the president and general manager of Magic Chef during our time together early in my professional career in West Tennessee.

I hope my younger readers are noting a trend emerging as I move forward in my career – pay attention to detail and glean all you can from where you are employed. You never know when a skill or practice that you encounter will come into play in another position in the future.

Contract packaging fulfilled the opportunity for a challenge that would tax my skill set in a way that would enable me to grow and succeed in the next phase of my career. It was during this time that the generational workplace started to take definition for me. I was in my mid 30s. I had calmed down and was no longer impatient for an opportunity to develop for me. I was becoming savvy enough to discern the intrinsic value attached to my pursuits and how it involved interaction with those on both sides of my current status. It positioned me to be where I wanted moving forward in my professional career. This aptitude galvanized my position at the time, but nothing lasts forever in my career, which is why I can identify with Millennials, perhaps more closely than others of my generation.

Chapter 6
The Seeds That We Let Grow

The Seeds That We Let Grow

The major player in the discount big box retail chain was exploring an opportunity to do business and proposed a packing proposition that upper management just could not refuse. Firmly entrenched in my status as the corporate quality manager, I was about to learn how contract packagers assimilated major customers. I had not been heavily involved in business recruitment, but I did rely on good customer service to help maintain a positive relationship and perpetuate the business.

Once the job bid had been approved, I found out that the retail chain had a "way" in which they went about doing business, which was referred to as power buying. In layman's terms and for the purpose of our business model, that meant that delivery of product was on a certain date or no delivery at all. Our entire workforce was about to experience unprecedented change to an already fast-paced, time-sensitive environment. This project came with a new packaging machine, a different set of packaging guidelines, multiple packing stations with moving equipment, and a prototype unit to be used until a project had been completed. The machine would run 24 hours a day, seven days a week until the product had been completely packaged. The company that made it sent a technician to help set it up and train the operators for use. There was also a large manual filled with prints and technical language.

I offered to sit in on the training sessions, but was informed that it was not necessary. The company had decided to train a 19- and 21-year-old. I learned a great deal about Generation X over the next couple of weeks. I spoke with the technician to get a few pointers on the new machine, and his pointers were primarily how to reference the manual. That conversation would prove to be of tremendous value just a short time later, as the implementation and completion of the project proved to be almost insurmountable.

Initially, I was directed to simply oversee the quality aspects of the new operation and let the "pros" handle the rest. I suspected that the two young operators would not hold up for the entire run of the product on 12-hour shifts seven days a week. I suspect that Millennials get their value of money from their parents. Generation X parents were never as driven as their Boomer parents. Boomers planted the ideology in the mind of our offspring that we would be dedicated to making sure we provided for their needs, wants and desires. We gave them opportunities to dream big and pursue the American dream with a college education and tailwind at their backside. They could rely upon our sage wisdom and advice to steer them through the rocky times. I think we may have missed the mark a little on that one.

After one of the trained operators walked off the job without giving notice, I became a part of the management team that stepped in and began to lead by example. I always had a soft spot for a challenge, so I accepted the gauntlet that had been given to me. To my credit, I succeeded in getting the quality standards and metrics up to acceptable levels for our primary customers and could fully dedicate my time to the new challenging project.

You look through a different lens when responsible for production as opposed to quality. This project set the stage for my first interactive generational workplace experience with Millennials. These were the very young Generation Xers that displayed work characteristics worthy of their Baby Boomer grandparents. They possessed a mindset that I was able to work with in order to successfully meet the deadline before us.

The Seeds That We Let Grow

We had a rate that was initially applied to the operation in order to meet the hard production deadline per the customer's requirements. Because the machine rarely ran continuously, my first objective was to determine the root cause of its intermittent downtime. It was causing the cushion built into the project to all but vanish.

With the lukewarm approval of upper management, we began to walk before we could run. We did not meet the production metrics, but the machine was producing product continually over a 24-hour period. Within a short span of time, the machine began producing the numbers that were projected per day. Due to the repetitive nature of the operation, I cross-trained my crew so that no one became too overwrought with their tasks. We had the night shift, and we made it a daily goal to out-produce the day-shift crew. Soon, the day shift trained another operator, and being an older gentleman, he asked me how we seemed to get more done in the same amount of time. I gladly explained that the young folks on my staff responded to praise, camaraderie and transparency. I strongly suspect that Millennials in the generational workplace of today would respond in similar fashion.

One thing I learned about the chaotic world of contract packaging was that, once a plan began to fall into place, it was a very satisfying process to behold. I learned a great deal that summer, and once the project had come to its fruition successfully, I was ready to return to my former assignment as corporate quality manager. I had finally joined a company that actually appreciated the skillset I brought with me and found other ways in which to challenge my abilities.

I had to reconnect with those at the appliance distribution warehouse, which was in Milan along with our satellite facility, which did most of their packaging. This was a stage in my career where I was not only gaining value, I used the majority of the skills I had accrued over the years to apply wisdom to the experience. Later in my career, I would discover that the term commonly applied to what I was doing was tacit knowledge. I want the younger reader to take particular note of this entry, as the relationship I established with a previous employer with the same management team would serve me well in their own company.

The parent company was operating smoothly and efficiently; however, such could not be said of the subsidiary. The parent company president and general manager were making frequent visits to the subsidiary, but problems continued to occur.

I was tasked to go to the subsidiary to find why it was continually losing money.

My presence in the subsidiary was not openly embraced by its management staff. I trained someone to oversee that the operation performed well, but I found out that, due to the variety of product that was being packaged, she was overwhelmed. When I spoke with the plant manager about the potential for problems, as well as additions to the quality staffing, I was informed that the plant's budget for indirect labor would not accommodate it.

I understood the math, but was puzzled as to how he managed to convey that to the parent company. I knew that the company president was an austere individual. I proceeded to speak with supervisors and lead personnel throughout the subsidiary, and I was more than a little distressed that a clear solution was not available to them at that time.

After completing my two-day visit, I submitted a

The Seeds That We Let Grow

proposal to initiate a positive change in the subsidiary. It was with some trepidation that I agreed to proceed as directed, as the last time I had gotten involved in such an activity, I had become a significant element of the solution. The meeting that ensued to review my summary opened the door for the greatest business challenge I had ever encountered. It would become the most satisfying and rewarding of endeavors I had ever been involved with in my entire professional career.

Chapter 7
All the Kings Horses and All the Kings Men...

One week before Labor Day, I was transferred to the subsidiary to be a production supervisor for the appliance customer's packaging department. I was tasked to turn that aspect of the business into a consistently profitable one. I had the liberty with the customer to initiate changes on the packaging side of the business, and I reported to the president of the company. Who could pass up an opportunity like that in an aspiring career that had already been substantiated by previous success at overcoming daunting challenges?

From the very beginning, I let my leadership style of empathy, honesty and humility shine through to all those on my staff. It was soon understood that there were two unacceptable answers to any question: "We have always done it that way" and "I do not know."

I had learned from the parent company that on many days in the packaging business, you must control the chaos. The subsidiary, however, had not received that memo. I found out quickly that the plant manager's field of expertise was the garment industry, and he was still trying to get a handle on the packaging business. To his credit, he was willing to allow me virtually free reign in implementing my ideas within my department.

In the first week I was onsite, I requested a meeting with all the people at Maytag involved with our operation to discuss issues, problems, and recommendations for improvements. They were gracious enough to invite me to their facility to meet with their plant manager, warehouse manager, shipping and receiving operations manager and the quality manager. I had done this in the past with the parent company with a good result. As it turns out, customers are very interested in their needs being met as a necessary element of doing continued business with them. I took three pages of notes on a legal pad and assured the staff that their needs would be addressed immediately.

The shipping and receiving manager was the only one to ask about the timeframe of delivery I had in mind, and I calmly informed her that, with her assistance, two weeks. To say she was skeptical would have been a gross understatement. She just smiled and made a note of her own.

Now it was time to have a meeting with my staff to relay the findings of my meeting with our primary customer and convey the expected requirements I promised to produce. I requested that they take ownership in our business and embrace the model that had worked well for me in the past. I urged them to work with me, as opposed to working for me, to accomplish the strategic plan that I had conveyed to each of them. I explained that, collectively, we could achieve the lofty goals I had set before us and perhaps even have some fun in the process.

My crew found out quickly that I would not be a sit-in-the-office type of leader. It is amazing how a group of people can respond to encouragement, proper guidance and sound direction in working towards a common objective. Sometimes, leaders have to state the obvious. Without customers, we have no business, benefits or gainful employment. The tensions I perceived when I wrote my proposal for the president were fading away rapidly on a daily basis. Same staff, different results.

I also received an interesting phone call at the close of business on Friday of the second week after my meeting with the customer. Actions speak louder than words, and a customer will respond to positive results almost every time.

All the Kings Horses and All the Kings Men...

The loudest naysayer from my customer meeting at Maytag had suddenly become an advocate. She called me Mr. Polley and asked if she could continue to expect a continuation of the impressive results she had obtained from our facility. I humbly replied that this is what they had hired us to do, and she could look forward to growing accustomed to the results that we had produced during that time frame. This was the beginning of a satisfying and mutually rewarding business relationship.

Surprisingly, my plant manager was only interested in weekly updates with a brief meeting in his office. He commented that he was pleased that he at least had one area of his plant that was showing signs of improvement and profitability. I offered to add some insight to other areas of the operation, but he said it was being handled. Clearly, he was not as familiar with the president of the company as I was.

I cultivated a good relationship with the members of my team and management staff within our department. I also established a productive working relationship with shipping, maintenance and quality assurance. I had some difficulty developing any type of repertoire with the supervision and support staff with the other department within the subsidiary. They were very disorganized and continually had problems locating product within our facility to package and send to the customer. They simply had no system in place to efficiently package that customer's product.

I offered them support and guidance, but since they lacked any sense of direction, they assured me that my assistance would not be required in their affairs. I turned my focus to the area I had been tasked to turn around and proceeded to make an impact simply by using my management style of empathy, honesty and humility. My staff's ages ranged from

I Am Not An **Anachronism** | Don Polley

18 to 61. From the start, I explained to my crew that I played no favorites nor did I wish to be patronized for my role as production supervisor. I assured my team that I would ask no one to do anything that I would not do or had done before.

People appreciate honesty and transparency in what is occurring in their workplace. I applied a principle that I was already familiar with; satisfied employees provide exemplary service; which translates into satisfied customers. In a relatively short period of time, I effected a cultural change within the department I had been assigned to oversee.

I thought that with the progress my team was making and the difference in their disposition as compared to the other areas of the subsidiary that I would become more involved in permeating the positive changes in culture throughout the plant. Once again the plant manager indicated that each area should remain autonomous and attend to their own way of doing business with their respective customer. It was at that point that I knew for sure why the satellite business was struggling to turn a profit for the parent company. I recall a meeting the plant manager had with the department heads at the end of October. He was excited to share with us that the plant had just achieved its best month of the fiscal year; we had broken even for the first time all year. I sat in stunned silence as everyone else seemed to be elated at the good news and thanked me for my part in making that happen.

Unfortunately, my team was not the problem, despite being part of the solution. Just as I had suspected, things were about to change not only for the management staff but for the entire operation. I had finally learned to have some patience in waiting for change to take place. For the benefit of my younger readers, sometimes it is necessary to curb your enthusiasm and wait for the appropriate time to unleash innovative ideas to effect a positive change. Not long after that meeting, I was invited to attend a meeting with our plant manager, the general manager and the president of the company.

      A position of authority not only comes with expectations, but also with accountability. Since I had history with both the general manager and the president of the company, I knew that the phrase "I don't know" would not play well with that particular audience. I would find out in another meeting why I had been invited to attend that particular staff meeting with upper management. It seemed as though my original evaluation of the facility had been spot on in regards to the problems that existed in the facility. In the next meeting, I was offered the keys to the castle with the accompanying stipulation that if the plant did not start making money within six months, then the operation would be shut down and incorporated into the home facility.

      I requested and received virtual autonomy for decisions made pertaining to what was to become "my" facility and was granted my request, pending the outcome of the corresponding results produced.

Chapter 8
Crawling from the Wreckage

The first order of business was to meet with the department heads within the plant. The next was to share the task before us with the entire plant. Servant leadership not only dedicates a leader to the success of his or her team, it endears the team to be receptive and responsive to the goals and vision of the leader. They all understood from that point forward that an engaged leader understands change, communicates effectively and supports employees through their uncertainties. I had managed diversity throughout my professional career in differing capacities, but the challenge before me at this point was on a grander scale than what I had accomplished in the past.

First, we needed to evaluate the relationship of direct to indirect labor and then adjust as necessary to restore balance and make an immediate improvement to the bottom line. I designated my hand-picked and personally trained quality assurance woman to be my production supervisor over plant-wide activity. To ease the transition, her primary focus was on the appliance packaging department. We had developed a good working relationship and had confidence and trust in our decisions; she was completely on board with the daunting task before us.

I eliminated the quality tech position with the approval of Maytag, the customer, by introducing total quality management to the packaging team, giving them accountability for what they packed. I found that when expectations are clearly defined, engaged employees will embrace the challenge, step up and deliver best results.

I emphasized to everyone that customer satisfaction was paramount if we were going to avert a plant closure and that each employee was an invaluable resource in achieving our objective as a cohesive team. I already had a good relationship with those within my department from when I was their production supervisor, but now I had to incorporate the same goodwill and cooperation from the other segment of the business.

I found that the other customer, Grinnell, regarded us simply as a vendor; they conveyed what they needed done, and we produced the results. I soon determined that their preference was to relay information about their packaging needs through our parent company in Dresden and were not particularly interested in feedback from where the work was actually done. I found that the supervision staff of the other department spent the majority of their time looking for product that was supposed to be in our facility for packaging. I surmised that much of the inefficiency credited to our facility was directly related to that aspect of the business.

Initially, my office was the last place you would find me because I was continually on the production floor assisting when necessary, enabling flow of work product and assessing areas in need of improvement. I found that there had been no continuity in staging of product from the other in-house customer as any discrepancy in numbers or product was caused by our inefficiency and unencumbered by any action on their part. My recommendation to the home office was that we eliminate the customer from our facility.

It requires confidence in your staff as well as your primary customer to make a proposition of that nature since a decision of whether to close the plant was getting closer. The customer sent a team from its plant into our facility with fork lifts, scales and everything they needed to do a comprehensive inventory of their entire product. This process took two days to complete, and no inbound freight was unloaded pending the result of the inventory.

The next day we received a call requesting that we check to see if we had any of a certain product to package and to ship back to them at once. The decision was made at that point not to accept any more freight from their company and package all products that we had in house back to the customer. Once the packaging operation was completed, any employees of that department were invited to stay pending probationary review for hire.

Not surprisingly, we had few takers because they felt our guidelines were too strict and they had no desire to get on board with a team concept. The appliance distributor was true to its word and supplied adequate business to enable our business to function smoothly and efficiently at a profit for the home company. The year 1996 was destined to be a profitable one for our satellite company; this trend would continue throughout the course of its operation.

As we eliminated the primary source of inefficiency in the plant, I could once again reconnect with the mainline business, Maytag. It would become our mainstay throughout my tenure as plant manager at the facility. The two chief elements of the external customer were satisfied: Our parent company was happy because we had become a profitable arm of their business and the customer had finally gained confidence in our ability to provide their packaging needs despite ever-changing product to be packaged. I had finally gotten my message across to them that **coordination + communication + cooperation** translated into **continuity** within the operation so that progress could be gauged at any given point in time.

Fortunately, my staff embraced the concept early on

so that we could collectively achieve the objective that was laid out before us from the very beginning. Management responds to results, customers respond to satisfaction, and the road I had traveled in my professional career to date had enabled me to share empathy with all points in the equation. When you combine sincerity with honesty to establish trust, you build a solid foundation for a relationship that can withstand peaks and valleys for the long haul.

This is where an understanding of generational diversity comes into play as a driver for success. Generally upper management is comprised of older and experienced decision makers, who are receptive to new ideas if they are convinced that it will produce results and add value to the overall operation. Front line supervision must be completely sold on the process, the strategy and the plan in order to instill ownership to the subordinate staff. I was a firm proponent of the team concept as a chain is only as strong as its weakest link. We were galvanized by the obstacles we had overcome to achieve success.

Continuous improvement was a common theme that ran throughout the facility, which had become such a vital part of my life and the focal point of my career to date. Each member of the production staff had unrestrained access to my attention and were very aware that my actions were geared toward their best interests. Initially, the budget had no room for employee raises, but I found other ways to offer rewards to acknowledge the staff's dedication to satisfying the needs of the external customer. I knew from past experience that if the internal customer was satisfied, external customer satisfaction was the natural progression of the business.

I made it a point each day to personally let my staff know how much I appreciated their efforts. Now, I find out that this is an element that Millennials desire, and I marvel that this had been an aspect of my leadership style since the seventies. I knew that salary increases were not available for a plant that had lost money for the parent company, but we still needed to make a profit. However, there are ways in which to reward a dutiful and diligent staff without increasing their take home pay. We worked in an old arsenal plant that was not designed for air conditioning and had boiler heat in the winter. When the temperatures soared outside, we would enable additional time to be added to breaks as the break room was air conditioned. It is amazing how an extra five minutes can be so well received as a perk to a supportive staff. Another benefit that I added in my first year as plant manager and continued throughout my tenure was to have a potluck meal about every six weeks. I provided the meat for the meal.

My workforce was primarily women, and we had some outstanding culinary chefs on staff. When we had our potluck meals, I extended the lunch break 15 minutes to allow for fellowship and camaraderie among the staff. The stipulations were that no one could smoke in the break room for the benefit of the non-smokers and everyone was to be at their work stations promptly at 12:45. These gatherings enabled us to establish a family-type atmosphere in our workplace and also allow each of us to gain a greater appreciation of our coworkers. I encouraged frequent unannounced visits from the appliance distributor's warehouse manager, and he once arrived during our Friday dinner. He informed me that if I did not let him know when we were going to do this again, he would make adjustments to the workload in our facility.

He and I had a great working relationship. The fact that the customer was invited to visit our facility at any time promoted confidence. I had accomplished what the parent company had tasked me to do in six months with the help of

I Am Not An **Anachronism** | Don Polley

an exceptional supporting staff and development of a positive and enduring relationship with our primary customer. I had also learned many years earlier that it was a good idea to establish a positive relationship with your vendors to enable you to focus on more pressing matters during stressful high impact periods in the course of a business cycle.

I was very fortunate to have the great pleasure of working with such a vendor at the parent plant. He was especially helpful and supportive during the debacle with the new packaging machine, and he became a valued friend and trusted resource as I settled into my role as plant manager of the satellite facility. His familiarity with the inventory of packaging materials was invaluable to me as the previous management staff kept little or no records on which we could base future orders.

Once you establish a bond of trust, understanding is a natural by-product to those interested in a mutually satisfying business relationship. This was just another example of cashing in on the value I had gained at a previous career stage. This particular vendor enabled me to save hundreds of dollars each year on packaging materials and supplies and was always available to do whatever was necessary to insure that we did not run out of anything we needed to get the job done for our customer. For the benefit of my younger readers, this is the type of business relationship you can develop in person and by verbally talking on the phone. Despite ending our business relationship over 17 years ago, we are still friends today. If given an opportunity to push any business his way, I would not hesitate to do it as he is just as diligent, dutiful and focused upon customer satisfaction today as he was then.

Chapter 9
Earning Recognition

I Am Not An **Anachronism** | Don Polley

Now that the customer was satisfied and the staff was beginning to gel and settle in for the long haul, it was time to address the big picture.

After six profitable months in a row, upper management responded with raised expectations. When such a development is aligned with your own intentions, the result is simply a natural progression of achievement.

If I had learned anything over the course of my career, it was that nothing lasts forever. I had experienced somewhat the career path of a Millennial without the benefit of an MBA and a smartphone. Experience is the best teacher as there is no substitute for having a frame of reference upon which to base a decision that has a significant impact upon the business with which you are currently involved. Gaining value is all about being cognizant of the core issues upon which you based your decision. When you are able to properly discern the context that led to the reasoning used to respond appropriately, then you learn how to respond proactively instead of reactively to a situation.

The context of my situation was easy for me to assess. I had begun my career as a leader by waiting until I turned sixteen so I could be promoted to assistant manager. The workforce I was to lead so many years before was comprised of those entirely older than I was, but they respected my drive and initiative that enabled our store to prosper and gain recognition within our district. Even then I was learning how to manage generational diversity in the workplace.

This was my first big experience with Millennials. I could see the big picture because I had learned to share empathy and how to relate with all members of the workforce, regardless of their age. Four generations were working at the plant: Traditionalists (who had been my initial mentors and role models), Baby Boomers (of which I was a member), GenXers and finally Millennials. I could not foresee that this experience would actually benefit me 20 years later, but I had already become accustomed to gaining value at every career stage.

When placed in a position of authority in a situation that is beset with problems, it is necessary to enlist the aid of everyone involved to take ownership and embrace the vision of the desired outcome. This requires that employees respond to change and learn to adapt to an evolving workplace that presents new and different challenges each day. Such is the world of contract packaging; having a flexible workforce was contingent upon achieving and maintaining success. Once we attained consistent profitability, it was vitally important that we closely monitored our ratio of direct to indirect labor. With the approval of the parent company, we initiated a program that was to become a mainstay throughout the course of my tenure as plant manager. It became both a benefit and a reward for the diligent associates of our team. Millennials of today are looking for flexibility in their work schedules. We had done that successfully in the mid to late 1990s with a hybrid of such a concept. I coined the term VLO, for voluntary layoff. Employees could take time off without being subject to being penalized for an absence.

Initially I based this added perk on seniority. It was not written procedure so I had some latitude in how to apply it as long as no one complained or took issue. Since I had established a bond of trust with my staff, they relied upon my fairness to properly implement this new program. It is amazing that once people feel that they are involved in how their place of business operates, they become engaged in the outcome and interested in overall success of the business. Based upon the success I had achieved throughout my professional career, I found that an engaged leader will promote an engaged workforce. My leadership style was basic; today it is referred to as servant leadership. I used empathy, honesty, and humility to initiate a strategy of communication, cooperation, and coordination to get the job done. When asked to share the secret to my success, I first credited the employees and their acceptance of the 3 C's (coordination, cooperation and communication) business model to successfully achieve their objectives and goals. Year one would set the foundation for a satisfying and productive tenure as plant manager in a money-making facility.

The second year proved to be challenging because we had raised the bar of expectations high during year one. We had become a business unit at that point. I was confident that we could be achieve any objective that upper management at the home plant would channel our way. That philosophy worked for me, but I would need a "carrot" to entice the staff to step up because they were beginning to feel that their best efforts were not being rewarded financially. Smiles were commonplace in our facility, tardiness was a rare event, and absenteeism, once a problem, was now very manageable. This could be attributed in large part to the voluntary layoff element that had been implemented into our operation module at the satellite facility. Sometimes one has to think outside the human resources manual to create a perk that is regarded as a reward and universally acceptable to all parties involved.

We managed to go from a facility that had a reputation of poor working conditions and high turnover to one of being a decent place to work with low turnover. Creating an atmosphere conducive to a stable workforce enabled us to benefit the parent company in many ways. An engaged workforce satisfies customer needs as a byproduct of coming to work. In addition, we won an award from our insurance carrier for zero lost-time accidents, which was to become an annual award for our facility. Working safely and productively will put a facility in a positive light with its parent company every time.

I learned a great deal about myself and my management style during this period of time. I realized that the lessons learned in the past had application in the future. Managing generational diversity was just as important as any cultural or gender-related diversity issues that create conflict in the workplace. The solution could always be applied to a misunderstanding of the inherent issues at hand. Resolution generally was a simple matter of building a bridge of understanding to achieve clarity for all parties involved to achieve a common goal or objective. Once you build a relationship based upon a foundation of trust and understanding, communication becomes an integral part of the daily routine, and understanding becomes a natural by-product of adding clarity to the equation.

The next step was to secure financial rewards for the staff's dedication and diligence. Together we had increased productivity, slashed indirect labor, reduced variable costs, and come together as a workforce to enable a family-type atmosphere to our operation. After over two years of producing significant gains and profit for the parent company, the staff was rewarded with a somewhat significant increase in pay. Ordinarily, I loved it when a plan came together.

However, the pushback on the pay increase was somewhat significant as it was not as large an increase as anticipated. Despite my best efforts to indicate that it was a generous increase in pay, there was a short period of discontent before reason ruled the day once again. I was fortunate to have employees with an average age of around 33 on staff at that time. Millennials were just entering into the workplace and were compliant with the majority as they were testing their expectations and gauging their talents as they began their career. I can relate to them because it was around this period that I purchased my first personal computer for home, work and school. I still recall declining a company cell phone as I felt it was unnecessary for me to have one to do my job. How times have changed.

Chapter 10
The Jaded Edge

I Am Not An **Anachronism** | Don Polley

The surprising reaction of my staff to the pay increase they had worked so hard to achieve caused me to reflect upon what we had accomplished together under my leadership and guidance. What we learned to do as a collective group each day was to embrace the challenges of a daily "hot load" from our customer of product that had to be packaged that day. We got that done in less than ideal working conditions both safely and productively. You learn the lesson in the past; you apply it in the future. I learned that the implementation of the 3 C's, which had been so effective in the 1970s, still had application in the 1990s. To be effective, it has to be implemented by an engaged workforce that agrees with the vision and focus of the leadership team.

We were able to build a relationship of trust and understanding among staff members despite gender, age, ethnic and cultural differences. We worked together to manage diversity in our workplace and avoid potential conflict and oversight. Accountability is not hard to trace when it begins with those in charge and filters down to every individual taking ownership of their part of the overall success of the operation. I may have received the accolades from the parent company, but I always pointed to the fact that my staff accomplished the heavy lifting and made it happen one day at a time.

The three C's of coordination, cooperation and communication that had worked so well in the subsidiary were not as well received by the parent company. Two out of three was unacceptable to me. In the domain of my plant, however, when dealing with the "home office" there were occasional lapses in the application of such a tested philosophy. Fortunately, success generates a currency that can be translated into leverage if used properly and applied tactfully. I managed to get a raise for my staff, but I met with resistance when I requested a benchmark or guideline by which I would be able to increase my salary or benefits with the company. Tracking where you have been helps you understand the obstacles you have overcome and provides you with some definition for future accomplishments. Adding value is always a worthwhile pursuit and one that begs merit if it results in the achievement of a lofty goal.

    A combination of events in both the personal and professional aspects of my life led me to make some choices that would leave an irrevocable imprint on my life from that point forward. Declining to enumerate the personal tragedies that I encountered during my last year as plant manager, in conjunction with an extraneous sequence of events that would disrupt the continuity of the subsidiary from outside pressure from the parent company; we managed to weather yet another storm. Once again an additional customer had come and gone as we remained bruised, but not broken by the event. This time I was adamant in my request for an increase in salary; much to my dismay, I had to go elsewhere to find satisfaction to my request. Another packaging concern in the area with a distribution center had been encouraging me to come in for a visit for quite some time. Presented with a most intriguing and attainable offer, I made one of the most difficult decisions in my professional life and changed jobs.

    At 41 years of age, I had managed to make my mark in an industry that had few who were willing to pursue the path of servant leadership in order to achieve success. Subsequently it came as no surprise to me that my new staff was eager to embrace the changes in their operation in order to remain competitive. For once, upper management seemed to be onboard with the changes that I initiated to achieve customer satisfaction. Since I had already established a positive relationship with the customer, I was tasked with modifying the way in which business was being done in order to achieve success.

To my surprise, the primary customer was not the appliance distributor, but a parts distribution center located several miles away. The proposition I had bought into was that the appliance distributor was contemplating consolidation of outsourced packaging to one vendor. My new company had several other distribution centers in other states. I was told they would be committed to becoming the vendor that the appliance distributor chose, and I would be the selection as plant manager for such a facility with a significant increase in salary. Due to the impact of the personal loss I had experienced, I felt that having laser focus upon a career would be a good move for me at that time.

Gaining value at every career stage is comprised of learning many elements pertaining to the particular situation in which you find yourself, as you move forward with your career. Initially, I found my surroundings to be cleaner, more modern, and equally capable of accommodating the needs of the customer. Instead of being the plant manager, I was now a production supervisor; one of many who were on staff in my new facility. I managed to make a favorable first impression on my peers as the workload increased from the first week. One of the departments gained more billing as I had an influence on the type of product that required packaging from the woodshop. This caused an increase in billing for both departments. The numbers were significantly increased from the previous year from the very first quarter. I soon discovered that there was a bit of a rivalry among the supervisors for the other customer in house. The plant manager kept my department insulated from such nonsense for the most part as his bonus check had risen as a result of my hire to his facility.

Despite having won over my departmental workforce rather quickly to continuous improvement and customer satisfaction, I had apparently not disappointed regarding the reputation and notoriety that I had achieved prior to joining their team. Unfortunately, the same goodwill did not play well with my colleagues, as they seemed envious of my positive relationship with upper management in addition to the success I exhibited consistently in sales gains for the company. I thought this to be a bit odd, but I was the "new kid" on the block and had not built the repertoire that generally comes with longevity. They seemed to resent the cohesiveness that our branch of the operation displayed as we were housed in a separate building adjoining the main plant. It was not unusual to see my employees smiling and cutting up with each other at the end of the day. I shared the 3 C's with them as well as the upside of using servant leadership, which they perceived as my meddling in their affairs. Much to my chagrin, I was being drawn into the politics of the operation.

The decision to consolidate outsource packaging to one specific vendor was in full stride by the summer. I had convinced the distribution company to enable me to start a second shift operation in order to display to the appliance distributor our capability to accommodate additional workload. Since I had been instrumental in working with a team of exceptional employees to avoid a plant closure, I felt this task would be much easier to accomplish because I had an exceptional team at this facility as well. One of the invaluable lessons I learned from this experience is that engaged leaders promote engaged teams, which embrace the vision. As you light the fire within them to achieve an objective, they know they have your confidence in their ability to deliver intended results. By the beginning of fall, I could see the direction of our efforts and began to eagerly look forward to the outcome of the decision after the first of the year.

I Am Not An **Anachronism** | Don Polley

My focus had been on results – increased business, increased profits, customer satisfaction, of both the internal and external customer. I was virtually unaware of the discontent caused by the uniformity in billing I had initiated at the approval of the plant manager as one of the guidelines to assist in helping the customer make its final decision. One of the biggest discrepancies I had noted when moving to the new distribution company was that the billing was inconsistent for similar product packaged in the same carton or container. I felt that continuity in this regard would help the customer more accurately assess the cost estimates contributing to its decision. I was unaware that the billing clerk was making an issue as if it would cause the company to lose money.

Billing and profits were at all-time highs pertaining to the appliance distributor primarily because of an increase in volume; they were not impacted by any reduction in margins as applied to billing. My best efforts were being impacted by pettiness and politics, two elements I was not accustomed to having to contend with. While in the process of addressing this issue, the plant manager had become embroiled in some manner of controversy that ended in his termination for reasons unknown to me at the time. The general manager was released as well. I found myself in a critical phase of finalizing the strategy for the successful completion of the business plan we had enacted together, without the support and guidance of my biggest advocate.

The new plant manager was young, inexperienced and unfamiliar with the product, the position and West Tennessee. His uncle was the president of the corporate distribution company. I had been around long enough to see how this was going to affect my career. Once again I had achieved success in a short span of time, but the impact upon my career was somewhat less than anticipated. The new plant manager informed the appliance distributor that the other customer in house was his main focus. This put me in an unfavorable light when the appliance distributor went with the competition as its sole outsource packager. My company offered me an opportunity out of town when it eliminated my position after we lost the contract with the appliance manufacturer. I respectfully declined. Just a short time later, the appliance distributor's main company sold out to Whirlpool appliance manufacturing, which did not outsource packaging. Ironically, at this stage in my career, I had been affiliated with and left that particular appliance company twice in the span of 20 years.

Chapter 11
Now You See What You Missed

Now You See What You Missed

It's funny how a devastating upheaval in your personal life can somehow buffer the impact of a life-altering event in your professional life. When I left the distribution center and its parent company, I knew it was going to take some time for me to readjust my personal compass and settle upon a direction for the next phase of my life. It was during this timeframe that Goodyear, the company I had tried to get a job with, contacted me to gauge my interest in joining their team as an associate.

Since I had gone through several of the "phases" involved in the hiring process two years before, I reasoned that this would give me an opportunity to explore the prospects of obtaining a management position with a Fortune 500 company. My motivation for getting hired was much different than it was in 1976 when I had first sought employment with this company.

My aptitude test placed me in a position to be a tire builder. I found this interesting because I submitted a copy of my resume along with my application upon re-entry into the hiring process. However, since I had recently divorced and was paying child support, I needed a job, so I took the offer. Any preconceived notions I had about working for the company were soon dismantled. I had to experience my new environment to truly appreciate what it was really all about. The culture was completely removed from what I had grown accustomed to in contract packaging. I had no idea how micro-managed the facility operated and wondered how in the world they ever got anything accomplished. Having worked with Millennials in a different capacity, I can understand why that type of management style would be particularly distasteful to them.

69

I Am Not An **Anachronism** | Don Polley

I always maintained a different perspective of what took place at that time due to my extensive background in quality and supervision. Since I was hired to be a tire builder, I set my mind on becoming the best tire builder I could be. I knew that one's reputation with a company begins from day one. I acknowledged the importance of gaining value at every career stage, and it was vitally important to establish good relationships with those who were a part of the value stream. This attitude enabled me to forge lasting relationships with both production control staff and area managers throughout the plant. Those relationships would prove to be invaluable during my career at the tire plant in West Tennessee.

Initially I had been hired in at 70 percent of top pay with increases of 5 percent at six-month intervals until I reached top pay status. We were working 12-hour shifts to keep the plant operating around the clock. I had to adjust from working strictly days to working nights from 7 p.m. to 7 a.m.

One of the benefits of being a tire builder was that one could work overtime almost at will, which in my situation enabled me to obtain the money required to satisfy the constraints on my life as stipulated by the ruling of my divorce. It was actually beneficial to me to be involved in earning a living performing a labor intensive job. I ended up working six days a week despite the work schedule. This gave me two, three-day weekends each month. I was an R-2 tire builder, which meant I was part of a two-man team. I found myself working with a variety of more senior builders who had different methods and styles of performing the job.

I learned a great deal working with different builders on different shifts. I also learned the tendencies of different area managers in different sections because when you were on overtime, you had to bid on a machine and work with the home builder of that particular machine. I became known as "toothpick" because I was constantly chewing on a toothpick as I did my job. I displayed a solid work ethic no matter where and with whom I worked. This enabled me to gain a solid reputation among other builders on both shifts, area managers and production control staff. I soon learned which builders to work with if I wanted to work hard and make money and which builders to work with if I did not feel up to putting forth maximum effort. In either case, I was regarded as being a welcome addition when working overtime. I discovered somewhat of a fraternity existed amongst builders in the tire room.

It is not without some trepidation that a company man acclimates to the guidelines of expectation in a union-operated facility. I noted a manipulation of the system from both sides of the spectrum throughout the course of daily operation. Since this was to be my livelihood, I resolved to fit in the best I could without compromising my character or personal integrity. Recounting the events of that period of time would require another book, a project for another time. I became acclimated to piecework and finding creative ways to build up my average and contribute to my personal bottom line on payday. Multiple generations were at work in the facility, making the capacity to be able to work with generational diversity a valuable commodity for both staff and supervision. Even in the midst of three thousand employees, I gained a reputation of being distinctive and unique in a short period of time. Having achieved notoriety among my coworkers and managing to earn a healthy pay, I found out that in the realm of production on that large a scale, things were bound to change over time.

The parent company decided to invest in the Tennessee plant. A new wave of tire machines was introduced and

I Am Not An **Anachronism** | Don Polley

implemented. Changes in the market share dictated adjustments in the volume of the facility, which led to a layoff. Had it not been for a national tire recall from a competitor, the layoff would have affected me sooner that it inevitably did. Another element in the facility was a capability to "surplus" labor from one business segment to another in order to maintain the needs of the business.

After one of my three-day weekends off, I discovered that not only had my machine been removed, but I had been surplused to work as a tire inspector in the final finish department. I discovered that it was a whole different world on the other side of the wall. It was beneficial that I was a tire builder before being transferred to tire inspection. I managed to acclimate to the new job quickly and effectively, despite the reduction in pay and the increased heat from working so close to the tire presses.

Surprisingly, I found that opportunities for overtime were available in my new surroundings as well. When gaining value at every career stage, one learns that it is essential to truly listen to what those who are experienced at performing the assigned task. It is generally to your benefit to take the tacit knowledge and apply it in order to build good relationships with your peers. A job well done will reap its own rewards. I caught on quickly and was allowed to work overtime. I knew that after the first of the year, the next layoff would catch me as well. When one does well despite working with adverse circumstances, others take notice and you never know when that may be of benefit in the future.

During a rare moment of downtime, a senior hand in the department shared his story with me, which enabled me to look at my situation from a different point of view. He was hired at the plant in 1975. During his tenure at the facility, he was laid off, surplused, on strike, married and divorced three times, and purchased five homes. (He clarified it was actually four homes because he repurchased one that he lost in a previous divorce.) As he recounted his past experiences, he jokingly told me not to worry too much about what I had missed from not hiring on in 1976. I pondered the irony of his tale as I had hired in on the throes of a divorce and was on the verge of a layoff – and 2003 was a labor contract year for the company. We were told that after the layoff, the chance of a recall in the future would be slim.

Chapter 12
Two Scoops

So here I was, 45 years old and just laid off from a job I had wanted since I was 18. I was forced once again to determine what I was going to be when I grew up. It was at this point that I could empathize with the Millennial generation as they were frequently accused of "job hopping." My work status had been completely beyond my control. As a part of the layoff agreement, I was offered an opportunity to go to school and retrain for a different career. When I accepted employment at Goodyear in Union City, it had never occurred to me that it would open a door of opportunity for me to explore academic pursuits beyond the walls of the tire plant.

After weighing my options, I decided to pursue an associate's degree at a community college at the expense of Goodyear and the State of Tennessee. Ironically, this was the same degree I had started to obtain in the late seventies and did not complete so I could earn a living and explore other career options. I found that your resolve becomes more focused once you have had years of experience and you wonder what might have been if you stayed the course.

Knowing that computer technology would be the wave of the future, I took three classes online. Fortunately, the one I selected to take on campus was introduction to computers. I did not own a computer and had very little experience online, other that using the network provided in house at Goodyear. I soon discovered that my computer skills were sorely lacking; so the challenge that was laid before me was a worthwhile endeavor. Gaining value at every career stage involved this aspect of my career as well.

I marveled at the apparent ease in which the younger students processed the information presented in class. It dawned on me that Millennials were a tech-native genera-

I Am Not An **Anachronism** | Don Polley

tion, which would have an impact upon their outlook in their approach to a suitable career path and their outlook towards the future. Had it not been for the aid of some of my younger classmates, my instructor and a particular lab assistant, my academic efforts might have been derailed right out of the gate.

    As I moved forward successfully in my academic pursuits, I began to realize that the younger generation (Millennials) learned in a different way than I did. During my first semester at the community college in the seventies, every desk had an ash tray. Laptops and smartphones did not dominate the academic landscape in 2003. I taught myself to be receptive to learn as the Millennials learned. I focused on my purpose, engaged with those who were genuinely interested in my development, and kept an ongoing conversation with my mentor to concentrate on my strengths in order to achieve my objective. My inherent penchant for empathy, honesty and humility was at work once again to enable me to succeed in school. It was during this timeframe that I recognized that the Millennial mindset was not so different from my own if I put it into the context of when I had started out after high school. Like me at the time, they were eager, adept and optimistic about the future.

    I had gone back to school in the early eighties and obtained an associate's degree at a community college in Southern Illinois in 1983. It was my intention to pursue a bachelor's degree from a nearby university so that I could work and go to school at the same time. When I shared my past experiences with the younger students, I discovered that many of them had jobs, families, and hopes and dreams for the future. It occurred to me that I must have the mindset of a Millennial. Despite the challenges presented by life's circumstances, they, too, were optimistic about the future. The main difference was their adeptness at accepting and acclimating to change. My generation, self-included, was more deliberate. I found that both generations, however, were diligent in their pursuits. Much to my surprise, I was able to relate to, empathize with, and interact with them as well as I did with any other generation that I had encountered over the course of my career. Perhaps I should have given closer thought to pursuing a career in teaching as my advisor had encouraged me to do.

I had been on an accelerated academic path, partly due to the credits I had earned from my previous academic pursuit and partly due to my choice of moving on in my career post-graduation. I was a single parent with a teenage daughter living at home, with both of us in school. I finished my requirements in December 2004, but was not awarded a degree until the next May. I discovered that the benefits that had supplemented my livelihood would stop when I completed the requirements.

I did not feel that right before Christmas was the best time to obtain gainful employment, but God is good all the time. I sent out several resumes in Fall 2004 and attended a job fair. A local company was sub-contracting warehousing and logistics and was in need of experienced fork lift operators. Much to my surprise, I received three job offers right before Christmas. The one that offered the biggest salary required that I go to Milwaukee, Wisconsin, for an interview. The second job wanted me to start immediately as a quality manager in a facility just outside of Memphis. It was a considerable drive from where I lived, but the salary was attractive and would have inevitably required a relocation closer to where I was to work. The least paying option was in a town that was the best option logistically.

I Am Not An **Anachronism** | Don Polley

After talking with my teenage daughter, I realized that her grades would suffer and she may not finish high school if I caused her to change schools in the middle of her junior year in high school. Sometimes the best choices are the easiest ones to make, as I had been influenced by my Millennial classmates in school to take stock in life and pursue that which is truly most important. Place the needs of your family first and pursue the option that best lines up with your career objectives. My daughter lost her mother during her freshman year in high school. She moved to Tennessee to live with me and go to school her sophomore year in a high school not far from where we lived.

My new company was Innogistics, a subcontractor to Procter and Gamble, one of the biggest employers in the area and one with an impeccable reputation in the community. Once again my leadership style would serve me well as I was soon made a dock lead on the north slide area of where I worked. Ironically, the hours were comparable to what I had worked at Goodyear under continuous operation, which involved 12-hour shifts. Still burdened with the financial requirements of my divorce, I worked overtime on frequent occasions. Maintaining a teenage daughter required creative funding at times. My penchant for doing whatever it takes to get the job done endeared me to the corresponding supervisor on the other nighttime crew.

On overtime I was tasked with cycle counting, shipping and filling in for other dock leads if they were absent. My computer skills enabled me to be able to move trailers to and from the yard, and we began shipping trailers from the north slide on the shift I worked on. Having the capacity to be able to understand and communicate across the generational divide helped me gain acceptance with the other subcontractors as well as the host company's support staff.

At this point in my career, I had given up any hope or prospect of being called back to work at Goodyear, so I was doing everything I could to distinguish myself among my peers. The general manager of Innogistics left for a better opportunity; the new general manager seemed to favor his own ideas over what Procter and Gamble wanted done. I witnessed a similar situation with the last contract packaging company I had worked with, so it was no surprise when Procter and Gamble severed ties with Innogistics.

P&G did provide an opportunity for anyone interested in working on the transition team (while P&G hired its own crew) to take an aptitude test, drug screen, background check and complete physical. This was similar to the process I went through to get a job at Goodyear in Union City. This is why it is so vitally important to gain value at every career stage, as you never know when what you have learned will be of significant value later on in your career.

Only a very small percentage of those tested were selected for the transition team. (I was one of them.) During the transition, all employees were put on the shift schedule that was used by the parent company. In less than two years, it seemed that my career path was to be substantially altered once again. I was hoping that my efforts on behalf of the subcontractor would get the attention of the parent company.

Spring 2006 presented me with career-impacting choices once again. The same week I was informed that I was on the transition team where I was working, Goodyear left a message on my home answering machine and a registered letter in my Post Office box. Due to the unorthodox schedule I was working, I had time off from Monday through Friday and had gone out of town. The notifications I received from Goodyear directed me to contact them immediately if I was interested in coming back to work in their facility. The key elements that led to my decision were the starting pay and three weeks of paid vacation as soon as I updated my paperwork to return. Once again I was going to be a finish tire builder at Goodyear in Union City.

I thought I had the opportunity to again get into a leadership role and have a chance to make a significant impact. I set my mind to facing the challenges that lay ahead for the transition team of which I was a part. My recall at Goodyear would consist of a six-week training program to become an R-3 tire builder. This was a one-man operation, as opposed to the two-man operation I had been certified in previously. Goodyear was in the midst of undergoing many changes in 2006, and the recall of those who had been laid off two years before was a harbinger of things to come in Union City. This was to be the second scoop of my tenure at Goodyear in Union City. I had successfully fulfilled my desire for a challenge with an opportunity to excel at my job, only in a different leadership capacity than what I anticipated. I had no idea what a roller coaster year 2006 was to be for me.

Two weeks into my training at Goodyear, my daughter gave birth to my first grandchild in Mississippi, and my mother asked me to take her to see the new grandchild. My request for vacation time took my area manager somewhat by surprise because I had just returned to work from such an extended layoff. I was granted 24 hours of vacation time which translated to two working days based on the 12-hour schedule the plant was on at the time. After I returned from my vacation, I found that my time in training was to be accelerated because I had experience building tires. Combining my leadership experience with the relative ease in which I worked with generational diversity in the workplace; I made the transition to again work at Goodyear somewhat seamlessly.

    Many of the associates in the tire room had assumed I had been surplused to a different department and not laid off. A lot had changed since I last had boots on the floor in the facility, and the tire room was a good place for me to start. Once again I encountered a bond that seemed to trace back to the opening of the plant in the late 1960s. This was to be the foundation of the second scoop, or second go around at Goodyear since being hired in 2000. Mindful of the advice given to me by the associate just before my layoff, I began to contemplate the future of my career and the role Goodyear was to play moving forward.

Chapter 13
Connecting the Dots

I was aware from the outset of my recall that 2006 was a contract negotiating year for our company, and the outlook for an agreement between Goodyear and the union seemed to grow less likely with each passing month. It struck me as odd that the contract would be negotiated in October after our busy season was over and during a period of normal slowdown in orders and demand for the product. Negotiating during a slow period would weaken the contract for the union. Additionally, the influx of recalled associates in the spring would contribute to uneasiness about the negotiations for a variety of reasons. Most had not worked in a union plant before and were unfamiliar with contract negotiations. To make matters more complicated, we had been brought in at a reduced pay scale that had been negotiated per the previous contract. I was already exposed to the impact of the changes in the operation from the contract that had been ratified the year I had been laid off.

For the most part, the labor union at Goodyear was an organization that deducted money from our paycheck for unsubstantiated value. However, those of us who did return to work after the extended layoff were able to distinguish the difference in our respective lifestyles before and after recall. Despite the fact that I too had been hired in at a reduced rate of pay, our group had the advantage of periodic raises every six months until we reached top pay for our respective designation or job title. The chief benefit provided to the new hires was cost of living adjustment increases, which had been negotiated into the contract language in the seventies.

I always looked at my situation through the lens of a leader in a boots-on-the-floor position, which enabled me to gain an interesting perspective on how to process the events that played out during this period of time in my career. I was

I Am Not An **Anachronism** | Don Polley

able to share empathy with both labor and management staff as I witnessed Goodyear's overall strategic plan for Union City unfolding. I perceived that a work stoppage or strike was inevitable due to the uncertainties and the lack of cohesion among the labor force at that time. I had been through a surplus, a layoff, and a strike was the only box I had not checked off during my tenure at Goodyear. The tire development aspect of our plant had been moved out; R-2 machines were being diminished and would soon be obsolete in our plant. The new machines were beginning to run productively, which was the parent company's intention from the outset when it invested in the Union City plant.

Over the course of just a few months, my situation went from the optimism that accompanies an opportunity to eclipse a new horizon to one of uncertainty that was caused by a work stoppage. The labor union and the company were unable to get together on a variety of issues. Concessions on the part of union-sponsored bargaining unit from the past two contracts had the rank and file membership apprehensive about the outcome of the ongoing negotiations.

I had been through a work stoppage while employed by the appliance company in Southern Illinois. I was much younger then. Having only two generations in the workplace at that time translated into a determination to make a statement and not give up any gains from prior negotiations. That was how it was then, but this experience was to be nothing like what I had encountered in the past.

The unity and definition of purpose that existed in the early eighties no longer translated to the new millennium. For the first time in the history of the plant in Union City, union members crossed the picket line. Union City had long been regarded as steadfast and a bold maverick with regards to negotiations among North American tire companies. No longer could Union City profess to claim such a distinction, and ratification would have a bittersweet savor despite the outcome of the negotiations. You learn a lot about people you think you know when their livelihood is put at risk and their future is cast into doubt and uncertainty. I suspected that once again the company would be in the driver's seat with regards to the outcome of the negotiations. What I had initially perceived as an opportunity to secure my future was evolving into a chance to gain value at every career stage.

The company had seen fit to bring in replacement workers during the time we were on strike in order to meet the needs of the company. It came as no surprise to me that the contract was accepted around the end of the year in December, replete with more concessions and accommodations to the company to meet the needs of the business. I understood at this point how I was hired in at a lesser pay scale than those who preceded me in the plant. I also understood the new Tool Kit, or "local improvement plan." The changes were a by-product of the concessions made in the 2003 master contract negotiations. Ironically, despite being laid-off, I had gone to the union hall and voted on that contract in 2003.

As a result of the contract negotiations in 2006, the plant in Tyler, Texas, was removed from the "protected" list of plants and the plant in Gadsden was to remain a protected plant. Due to a previous contract negotiation, Goodyear Union City per Article 53 was also a "protected" plant. When looking towards the future, it is best to gather as much information as possible in order to guide your career in the proper direction. Healthcare for retirees was moved from Goodyear responsibility to a Volunteer Employee's Beneficiary Association (VEBA). Employees hired after October 1, 2006 were to be under separate wage and benefit packages. The new hires would be saddled with many restrictions. I learned a lot about labor negotiations as I spent time at the union hall and manned the phone lines for those calling for information and to share their concerns.

  We had a meeting to vote on the new contract despite its shortcomings, the concessions made once again by labor and the proposed revised standards for any new hires. The contract was accepted, and we went back to work after the first of the year. Some of the replacement workers had been hired, and this caused some friction amongst the rank and file who had stayed out during the labor strike. By April 2007 there were many more new hires because orders were picking up. We discovered that the hiring process had been streamlined to decrease the amount of time between the interview and a job offer.

  Considering that Millennials were the generation born from 1980-1995, I marveled at the attitude and work ethic displayed by the Millennial new hires at that time. Clearly, Goodyear in Union City and, I strongly suspect elsewhere in North American Tire, was ill equipped to provide what was necessary to attract and retain Millennials. The Millennial employees had much difficulty adapting to the plant's micro-managing techniques and giving up two weekends a month to work as we were on a continuous-operation schedule at that time. I contend that one that has worked with and empathized with the concerns of the Millennial new hires could gain a good deal more insight than one could obtain from a textbook or class on the subject.

  Once again I found myself gaining value at this stage of my career. As time went on, the only ones that stayed were the older Millennials who essentially had adopted the whatever-it-takes work ethic of the Baby Boomer generation.

The same thing applied to the GenXers who hired in at that time, as they, too, seemed to have adopted the work ethic of their boomer parents. These insights in conjunction with my acquired skills of working in the generational workplace enabled me to connect with the new hires in a way that proved to be somewhat awkward for both management and union labor representatives at that time.

In order to have empathy, one has to be able to understand as well as comprehend the existing circumstances through the lens of those involved. I understood that the challenges faced by the new hires were more intricate than the challenges I had overcome years before when was I hired at the plant. They had to contend with not only the discrepancy in the pay scale, but also the difference in benefits from everyone else in the facility and the bias from the more tenured workers in the plant. Needless to say, for a time it seemed as though our shift had new faces every week. Over time, the new hires seemed to configure their own identity within the plant; for the most part they held those of us who made more money for doing the same work in relative disdain.

The R-2 tire machines that I was hired to run were being phased out as R-3 tire machines had been relied upon for increased production. In one section, elevators raised the finished tire up to a hook line that transported tires from the G-3 machines to the staging area to go to final finish. As it turned out, the plant had many areas in which the new hires could be placed and, with minimal training, could begin to make an immediate impact upon the production process.

In 2008, due to the economic slowdown in demand for tires, the Union City plant was placed back on an eight-hour shift with a six-day workweek. As it turned out, many of the more senior hands who had resisted the demands of continuous operation had become accustomed to having two three-day weekends per month. I was a tire builder at the time and welcomed the break from the rigors of a twelve-hour shift doing labor intensive work. I resolved at that time to never forget the stamina required to maintain high production standards under such labor intensive conditions.

 Due to my lack of seniority, I was still unable to transfer to the shift I wanted. At this point, the disparity forced upon the new hires was in full swing as management used the tool kit ramifications to enable them to coerce their subordinate staff into doing whatever they wanted them to do. The more senior area managers did not abuse this privilege, but others took advantage of the new hires' lack of experience and understanding. It is no wonder that the new hires felt that the union dues deducted from their paycheck provided them with little or no benefit. It would not be too long before they would find out the intrinsic value of their membership in the USWA.

 There is no way I could have ever gained the insight and experience of working with the generational workplace than the position that I found myself in at this time. Four generations essentially were working together at Goodyear in Union City, and I was about to experience the impact of the significant loss of tacit knowledge due to the implementation of the corporate office's strategic plan. In spring 2009, before the expiration of the existing contract, Goodyear corporate and our local union worked together to provide our local with what we would later refer to as the "Alford agreement," which was named after our local president at that time. Essentially it provided a buyout stipulation for the most senior employees. As a caveat of such an agreement, we had to agree to remove the plant protection provided by Article 53 of a pre-existing negotiation. It was at this point that the purpose behind the restrictions applied to the new hires per the previous negotiated contract would promote either disdain or indifference to such an agreement as they could see no benefit in it for them. For the senior employees, this gave them at least 600 opportunities to essentially either get out while the getting was good or take advantage of a chance to retire with full benefits based on service time as opposed to age.

Those of us in the middle were tasked with trying to reason with both sides about the future of the plant in Union City. Due to intense pressure from the local union representatives to ratify the buyout agreement, it passed by secret ballot in May 2009. The previous agreement expired in July and was twice extended before a settlement was reached. The new agreement took effect September 21, 2009.

As a result of the buyout, I was able to bid and transfer to the stock prep section of Goodyear and go on third shift. This was my preference since we had the conventional schedule of eight-hour shifts, six days per week. I found out quickly that things were done somewhat differently in this part of the plant as my resourcefulness as a tire builder was not well received in my new position.

Surprisingly the most friction I received was from the youngest member of our team. A GenXer, who had been put on the crew before the buyout, was given a hard time by the older hands on our crew. He seemed to feel that I needed to go through a "rite of passage" to work on their team. Once again my skill with generational diversity enabled us to resolve the situation without incident. Much of the ribbing I received was due to the fact that I had obtained two degrees from college and was still working at Goodyear. It turned out to be a good job, and I was fortunate to work with a great crew as it seemed that there may be a future for me at Goodyear

I Am Not An **Anachronism** | Don Polley

after all.

The buyout had left the plant with a void in tacit knowledge, but it seemed to galvanize the relationship of those of us who were left behind to deal with the uncertainties that the future would have in store for us in Union City. From my standpoint of having been in management as well as labor, it seemed that our plant had evolved into everything corporate had desired us to be. We were making our ticket; scrap was down as we began to coalesce into a smaller productive workforce at a reduced cost due to the disparity in pay for the new hires.

One thing I had learned from my tenure at Goodyear was that nothing remains the same; the winds of uncertainty began to swirl again when a new plant manager arrived in March 2010. He was the third plant manager at Union City since I started work there in 2000. He made it a point from the outset that he was not sent to close the plant down, but I felt that the writing was on the wall. To his credit, he had been the production manager in our plant during a time when we were a lot busier so he had familiarity with our facility as well as a degree of notoriety, but most of those most familiar with him had taken the buyout and were no longer in house to cause any disruption.

He was good at communicating with the rank and file; it was not uncommon to see him walking about in business centers throughout the plant, and he was accessible to those who had questions or concerns. The primary generational groups in the plant at that time were Boomers and Millennials, and they both responded well to the clarity of purpose that he emphasized during his time as plant manager. I began to note the similarities that existed between Boomers and

Millennials as we worked together to make the best of our situation.

 The new plant manager's premise was that if the marketplace improved, we may have a chance to avoid closure. At the same time, we had to reduce costs to gain the attention of the decision makers in the corporate office. We had come a long way in that regard, but knew there was still more to be done. Engaged leadership when focused on the common good inspires engaged leaders up and down the chain. This translates to an engaged workforce that can overcome adversity and significant challenges that lie ahead. I submit that the fate of our facility was no fault of the management or the staff that we had in place at that time.

 The new year seemed to bring a semblance of hope and promise as we had consistently met our production ticket. The plant manager said the numbers indicated that we were excelling in comparison with the other plants in Goodyear North American Tire. Union City had finally reduced the cost of production per tire to a level that was competitive within our group; this was accomplished despite a high volume of code changes we had to make each day. To put it in perspective, since we were making replacement tires representing many different models, the Union City plant had an average of more than 100 code changes each day, while every other plant in North American Tire had a minimal number each week. The economy was still struggling with recovery, the demand for new vehicles was down and there seemed to be increased pressure from foreign markets for replacement tires.

Chapter 14
The End of the Beginning

The End of the Beginning

I thought of the advice I received years before from the associate in final finish about the course of a career at Goodyear in Union City. I had been laid-off, surplused, recalled, on strike, and finally satisfied with the job I had so that I could feel confident about ending my career at Goodyear in good order. During my tenure at Goodyear I had occasion to work in different areas throughout the plant, which enabled me to determine which Business Center was the best fit for me. Because of the buyout, my new seniority standing in the plant would indicate that I did not have to be concerned with a layoff; I could contemplate settling in for the stretch run of my career at Goodyear. His advice was good, but it did not take into account an experience he had not had, but one that would alter my career decisions at Goodyear.

In February 2011, it was announced on Wall Street that Goodyear in Union City would be scheduled for shutdown by the end of the year. If I were to consider retirement from Goodyear, it would not be in Union City.

The news of the shutdown was conveyed by our plant manager to each shift; he did it in person with the same demeanor that he had displayed in other meetings at the plant. As stated previously, essentially two generations comprised the bulk of the workforce at that time. The older Boomers were shocked as they had been exposed to rumors of a shutdown throughout their careers at Goodyear; they had skirted the buyout believing that a plant shutdown was out of the question. Such news gets real very quickly when delivered in such a venue. Despite the news of a closure, our plant made its production ticket that same day. I wondered what the decision makers at corporate would think about that the next day. There was not much discussion among the rank and file as we began to contemplate the future. Suddenly the discrepancy in pay did not mean as much as where a paycheck would come from after the plant closed. By my estimation, I think the Millennials took the news in stride, and the Boomers had to come to grips with available options and life after Goodyear.

A job fair presented on all shifts for associates explored the option of moving to another plant in the Goodyear chain. There were pros and cons to consider as those who were younger and had service time could move to another plant until they either had enough service time to retire or reached retirement age. Many of the older Boomers in house had gone to other plants to work during the layoff, but they always had the prospect of recall to their home plant. Acceptance of a move in conjunction with company approval would require permanent geographic relocation. I considered a move to Topeka, Kansas, but was not entirely sold as to how Goodyear would hold up its end of the deal. During my tenure in Union City, I had seen how the transfers from the Dunlop plant in Huntsville, Alabama had been treated once they had agreed to sign away their right to return to stay in Union City. They were among the first laid-off in 2002 without regard to their service time in their home plant. Being a man of faith, I sought divine guidance before making a decision.

Ironically, another option for me was to continue my education with benefits and Goodyear assuming the lion's share of the tuition. My youthful dream of working at Goodyear had become a reality and now my desire to obtain a bachelor's degree from a four-year college was about to be fulfilled as a by-product of my acceptance of a job offer at Goodyear. It was not commonplace to include academic achievement in the same sentence with Goodyear Union City.

The End of the Beginning

It was during this time that I found myself relating to the Millennials as they began to regard Goodyear as just another stepping stone in their career path. Many of the Boomers had a gloom and doom ideology, while Millennials, for the most part, were just wishing Goodyear would set a firm closure date so they could plan accordingly. It began to settle in that I would be over 50 as I once again began a new chapter in my career path. I knew it would be a risk to pursue academics and graduate in my mid-fifties, but it was a chance I was willing to take. Much like the Millennials I talked to at that time, I had no lack of confidence in my ability to succeed. The chief difference between their ideology and mine was that I had experienced success in the business world prior to my employ at Goodyear. I felt the need to get back to the core of my potential; leaders lead, which is what they are inclined to do regardless of the particular position of their career at any given point in time. I found that I had lead by example during my time at Goodyear as many of the associates I had worked with had come to me for guidance, counseling and support as our livelihood was being compromised by a company that showed its appreciation for our efforts and dedication by eliminating our positions.

Ironically, I began my career at Goodyear after losing my job at the packaging company where I had invested much time and effort into its success and more than doubling its gross sales in less than one year. My reward was seeing my position eliminated for reasons beyond my control. Despite my best efforts to achieve high marks for overall customer satisfaction, the packaging company did not get exclusive packaging rights from the company I worked so hard to get. Now, after more than a decade of due diligence on behalf of a new employer, enduring the pitfalls and overcoming challenges along the way, I had successfully achieved satisfaction by doing my part to protect the company's good name and perpetuate the brand. It seemed to me that the business world of the 21st century would be much like the business world of the 20th century.

Overcoming the personal tragedies that had altered the course of my professional career at the end of the nineties would enable me to have the strength of character, faith and confidence to face the challenges presented in 2011. The death of my mother in April, the closure of the plant in July, and pursuing academic success in August – all in the same year – was a lot to process.

As I began to reflect on the potential impact of my decision to continue my education, I found that my next step was to to formalize my curriculum. The uncertainties many of my Goodyear colleagues displayed helped me to appreciate the opportunity I had. I would know which direction my life would take over the next two years, and the result of my decisions would potentially open doors of opportunity for me as I moved forward in my professional career.

I had taken full advantage of the opportunity to experience the impact of a plant closure across the generational divide, to experience first-hand the resilience of those of the Millennial generation to the news and take particular note of how much they were like Boomers like myself as we faced the social and economic challenges of our time early in our careers. As I contemplated their similarities, it occurred to me that I had always been an exception to the standard rule throughout my professional career. I had experienced the effects of age discrimination in my late teens to early twenties – even from those of my own generation – because my leadership success was the beginning of my prowess with generational diversity. Fast forward 30 years and add two more generations to the equation, I had refined my capacity for understanding generational diversity to enable me to empathize with each one across the generational divide. I resolved that with this talent, my background and experience in conjunction with an up-to-date education would enable me to position myself for success for the balance of my professional career. Goodyear was simply another stage in my career in which I had endeavored to maximize the value that I had gained from the experience.

Due to my extensive experience with being an exception to the rule, my hope was that upon graduation there would be a place for exceptional leaders with a wealth of experience and tacit knowledge to prosper in the 21st century. I had learned how to connect with the Millennial generation, been a part of the Boomer generation throughout my career, and still maintained respect along with a desire to gain wisdom from the Traditional generation.

I did not lack confidence in my abilities, but I was somewhat concerned with my ability to engage and compete with the best and the brightest at the university to which I applied. I was accepted by a university in the area that had an impeccable reputation nationally for academic excellence. I was finally in a position to obtain an objective that I had set my sights upon when I graduated from a community college in 1983. The world was a different place, my generation had made a positive impact in the world since then, and I was convinced that I was not an anachronism, this was my time, and everything I had accomplished over the course of my career had led to this opportunity.

It was now time to begin the final phase of my professional career. I perceived that if my age were to somehow be regarded as a liability, then through my academic success, I would be able to convince any potential employer that I

I Am Not An **Anachronism** | Don Polley

could add value to his or her organization. I was counting upon one aspect of the business world that surely would have carried over into the new millennium; value triumphs over liability every time. I was eager to embrace the final stage of my professional career as I embarked upon a new beginning.

Chapter 15
Reconnecting

I Am Not An **Anachronism** | Don Polley

I was accepted into Union University's BSOL (Bachelor of Science in Organizational Leadership) program, which was an accelerated learning program for adults that was held one night a week off campus in its own building. The classes were from 6 to 10 on Mondays. In essence Union packed 16 weeks of curriculum into five weeks for most of the courses included in the program. I became a part of a cohort group that would essentially stay together until graduation. Needless to say, I was the oldest student in the class, and I continually sought to add value to our group.

The first semester in the program I adhered to the scheduled format, but in order to graduate within the two-year window I was allowed, it was necessary to add additional classes along the way. Once again I had to formulate a course of action to accomplish my goal before attending my first class in the program. It was no surprise to me that I was regarded as an exception to the rule, even at the university level. I was very fortunate to have the guidance and assistance from a very competent and caring staff. The recruiter who had compelled me to choose his school over many alternatives made himself continually available to me to answer questions and assist with any issue that might occur in my academic pursuits. I would undoubtedly have been overwhelmed had it not been for his direction and support.

I was an only child and deeply regretted that my mother had not lived to witness the tenacity I had to overcome the difficult circumstances in which I was placed in 2011. There is no question in my mind that I was guided by divine influence and direction. I had to get over my grief and completely sever ties with my past; though Goodyear would be helping me get an education, I had no chance of being recalled to my old job in Union City. Things are not always as they appear as the future is always a variable in our lives. This is just another reason why it is so vitally important to gain value at every career stage. This was a good lesson I tried to share with my Millennial classmates as we moved forward in our academic pursuits.

Having achieved two associate degrees in the past, I marveled at the skill with which our professors ushered us through the program. Each one possessed a skill set that was indicative to the course in which we were involved and managed to seamlessly integrate what had been placed in the syllabus into the accelerated class structure. Due to the group project nature of many of the classes, it helped to create a loose-knit bond with others in the cohort group as group assignments varied from class to class.

I began to acknowledge the changes that had taken place in the business community since my last involvement in management in the late 1990s. Mobile technology had taken hold and strongly influenced the way in which information was created and shared. I reflected back to my most recent academic pursuit when I was provided a home PC that connected to the internet through dial-up and had Windows XP as its operating system. I knew I required an upgrade to pursue academics at the university level.

Before entering the program, I bought a laptop with Windows 7 as its operating system and set up a 4G internet connection in my home. I noticed a big difference in how things were done in 2011 as opposed to 2002. I may have displayed characteristics of a Millennial throughout the course of my life, but unfortunately I was not born tech-native and I had to struggle with comprehension of things that my classmates took with stride.

I Am Not An **Anachronism** | Don Polley

I realized that many of the Millennial generation had difficulty relating to why we did not understand some of the means with which they solved problems. I had to explain that things such as Google, YouTube and hyperlinks were things I did not grow up with, but I now needed to be adept using them. With a little patience and tutoring, I got up to speed as quickly as possible. I discovered that Millennials were just as impatient with our catching on as we were with their grasp of concepts we were trying to incorporate upon them. This experience helped me to understand many of the breakdowns in communication in the generational workplace, as it was primarily due to a lack of understanding many times from both ends of the spectrum. I determined at that point that if I were to succeed post graduation, this "old dog" would have to learn some new tricks.

It was during my second semester that I integrated online courses into the mix in order to stay on course with my plan to graduate. By this time, my laptop and Windows 7 were no longer "frenemies;" I had begun to use them as being a useful tool moving forward in my academic pursuits. Much to my chagrin, Windows 7 for Dummies had actually been of some value to help me make the transition from XP to the new operating system. (My good friend from high school has continually tried to encourage me to switch to Apple products but I resisted as Windows is what I was accustomed to using.)

My online class instructor seemed to keep our class inundated in work, projects, papers and tests, in addition to grading our participation in the chat on the discussion board. I began to see how one could become immersed into such a venue as time seemed to be of little to no significance as we began to relate in the class began to relate to one another in the virtual world.

One of the most interesting revelations I took from this experience was that despite being in class with some of those also in the online class, any discussion of the online topic was confined to the virtual discussion board and not to be discussed in person. It helped to understand how a group of Millennials could be sitting together at a table and some of them conversing by text message. It was simply a matter of preference; they were not trying to be rude. Empathy had always been strength for me in any of my leadership roles, so it was necessary for me to gain a firm understanding of these communication techniques. I actually had the opportunity to meet some of my virtual classmates in person and form some lasting bonds.

After making the dean's list my first two semesters in school, I became haughty enough to try to take an elective class online over the summer semester as the BSOL program did not allow for a summer break. Due to some technical difficulties in getting started, I decided it would be unproductive for me to continue in the class as I was struggling with understanding the material, and this would have adversely affected my grade. I requested taking the class on campus in the fall semester so I could receive classroom instruction. I did not earn an "A" in the class, but received a much better grade than I would have received online.

As I walked into the building for the first day of class, I asked a student sitting on a bench where I needed to go. I politely waited for him to finish his business on his phone and in jest asked him what he did before he had a smart phone. His response was, "I don't know," and I realized he was not kidding. This was one of two classes I had on campus during the fall semester besides my BSOL curriculum, and I realized I would be immersed in a sea of Millennials.

I Am Not An **Anachronism** | Don Polley

Not to overlook a potential opportunity, I found myself talking with the Millennials before class and asking as well as answering some very good questions. I found that the brightest Millennials were much like my own generation. As young people, we knew where we wanted to go, but were unsure as how to get there. Sometimes I think I learned as much or more in the hallways than I did in the classroom as I was gaining value at every career stage. I found the mindset of the Millennial to be most intriguing.

As 2012 began to fade into the past, I was still on track to graduate in Spring 2013. I was selected to be a part of the Vocatio program, which was offered to a select number of graduates to prepare them for success after graduation. I began to feel that I may actually graduate with honors. Initially I had some trepidation that I might not be able to compete with the brightest of the younger minds at the university level. Fortunately, the BSOL curriculum was geared toward a more vocational setting because many members in my cohort group worked and had children at home.

I was blessed to have the opportunity to pursue academics without having to work at the same time. This enabled me to step up on occasion when assigned to a group project and be available to dot the I's and cross the T's to help others in the group complete their part of the project on time. In return, my cohorts offset some of my technological shortcomings for the overall benefit of the team. Often, I have been designated as the group leader; once again my leadership style of empathy, honesty and humility was just as serviceable in academics as it was in the workplace. My extensive experience with working with generational diversity was an asset as well. I finally took my good friend's advice and procured an iPhone at the beginning of the spring semester in 2013. I thought my cohort group was going to throw a party as they proclaimed – some in disbelief – that the "cave man" had finally come out of the cave. It turned out to be good timing as I would rely heavily on its use and capabilities for a segment of the BSOL curriculum that was a particularly challenging group project towards the end of the semester.

I learned a great deal during my final semester. For example, I had an English class on campus that met only two days a week for one and a half hours. I was amazed at how many students missed that class. I didn't miss class because I didn't want to miss vital information and not do as well on the exam. I had always done well in English and naturally assumed I would have no problem with this class, and I needed to do well in order to achieve my goal of graduating with honors. What I failed to consider was that in my case anyway, no matter my age or how much education I had accrued previously, I was still susceptible to "senioritis."

At this university, you had to earn the grade if you wanted to make the grade. There was little margin for error if one aspired to achieve high marks. I was taken somewhat by surprise when I received a "B" in the first BSOL course of the New Year. I had not allowed for that in my calculations as I felt I had a good grasp of the subject material. This inspired me to redouble my efforts as I moved forward in the program. Still to come was what had been rumored to be the most difficult class in the BSOL program. It was a blended class with an extensive paper due at the end and a group presentation to the class.

Upon introduction to the class, my cohort group found the rumors to be spot on as we were in unanimous agreement that this one was the most challenging. The members of our group were pushed to our limit due to some unforeseen circumstances, but we stepped up and managed to pull together to achieve success in the end. In this instance, I was pleasantly pleased with the outcome of our combined efforts. However, the focus I applied to that class took away from a paper I had been assigned in English class. Not only was my premise off base, my grammar left a little to be desired. I was visibly stunned when I saw the grade I made on a paper returned to me during my mid-term exam. I was fairly confident that I had done well on it. My instructor, a published author, was kind enough to make time for me to see him in his office. I was given an opportunity to rewrite the paper and have the grades averaged, which enabled me to get a "C" for that assignment.

I could still graduate with honors but cum laude would be as good as I could do. Although not completely satisfied, I resolved to own what I had earned. The Vocatio experience was of limited benefit to me because I was the first who was accepted from the BSOL program, and, as I have stated previously, I was the exception – not the rule.

During a "mock interview" that was a part of the program, my mentor stated that they would have to create a position for me to fill. At the time I did not realize how prophetic her words would be as I moved forward in my professional career. It was just another example of the gulf of understanding that exists between Millennials and Boomers. Somehow we did not seem to connect on a level that would have been of maximum benefit to both of us. She was accustomed to working with the Millennial graduates who were accepted to the program. That experience is what helped me decide on the quote from Sir Isaac Newton that I use in my business material: "We build too many walls and not enough bridges." Had we managed to build a bridge of understanding, we could have accomplished so much more that would have been mutually beneficial to both of us.

I learned a great deal during my last semester at the university about myself, the Millennial mindset, and the impact of technology in academics, society and individually. Unfortunately, I had completely misjudged its impact in the world of business as well as in the generational workplace. I was excited to earn a bachelor's degree from such a distinguished university with a solid reputation in the community. I learned new strategies and techniques that would have been an unbelievable benefit to me earlier in my management career. I had learned that EQ was just as important as IQ in the business world; and my leadership style was still in demand in the 21st century.

There were essentially two key elements that I did not take fully into consideration as I prepared to re-enter the business world. I had not properly assessed the impact of the financial collapse of the previous decade and the ongoing recession. Both contributed heavily to the loss of my job and the opportunity to go back to school. I also failed to acknowledge the disadvantage that my age would present. Had I received the same degree before my tenure at Goodyear, my credentials would have been much more attractive and would have opened a door of opportunity to advance my professional career. I was confident that I would be gainfully employed within 90 days of my graduation.

Chapter 16
Rude Awakening

Essentially, I was continuously employed from 1974 to 2011. At any point in the past when I had to seek employment, I either responded to a phone call or filled out an application pending an interview for hire. I responded to an ad in the local newspaper for a job fair to take applications and interview for a position in 2004. I was also invited to visit a firm in Milwaukee, Wisconsin and I successfully made an impression on a company near Memphis that was in need of a quality manager.

Due to logistics, I had accepted a job in Jackson because I would not have to relocate and make my daughter change high schools so close to graduation. Much like Millennial parents, I opted for the benefit of family over financial gain. Empathy comes from an understanding of the sacrifices involved with overcoming challenges faced by others when confronted with similar life circumstances.

With my BSOL degree in hand, this was to be the last time I would need to seek employment.

I dropped off resumes at a job fair at Union University, which was as a perk of being selected to participate in the Vocatio program. It was offered to a select few of elite students in their field of concentration, which in my case was Organizational Leadership and Organizational Management. Though I had an opportunity, I did not take much time to speak to a recruiter who was in attendance. I did not realize at the time what an egregious oversight that had been, as now everything was done online and would be completely different from what I had experienced in the past. My smartphone was not ringing, nor were there any messages on the land line I still had. The virtual world of 2013 proved to be somewhat cold and indifferent to my approach of obtaining employ-

I Am Not An **Anachronism** | Don Polley

ment.

I found that when I submitted a resume and cover letter to apply for a position, I would instantly receive acknowledgement of receipt of my resume along with a "no-reply" that I would be notified of any interest in me at a later date. I did that over and over again. I wrote and rewrote my resume, watched webinars on how to write a resume and cover letter and kept stubbing my toe on a most unfamiliar term to me – key words. I began to peruse the online job boards, Career Builder, Monster and Indeed. I became so frustrated that I met with various temporary services in the area to see if they may have professional placements as well. At least they responded that they would let me know if they found anything suitable for me.

I had gotten to the point in my career that I had a wealth of experience. I had graduated with knowledge of the latest strategies and techniques for making a sound and significant impact upon any business. I had always been a leader, a mover and shaker. I always left each of my employers in better shape than it had been in before my arrival. I was eager and prepared to take the plunge into an opportunity in management, anxious to apply what I had learned and see how much value I could add to a new situation.

Millennials taught me to have a positive outlook and to look for opportunities to put my value on display and overcome the challenges presented in today's fast-paced business world. I found myself being ready and willing but somehow unable to find a job. The staffing services did call from time to time to offer me a job driving a fork lift for $10 per hour. I respectfully declined, thinking that something would open up for me in time. As Thanksgiving drew near, I decided to suspend my efforts to find a job until after the first of the year so that I could be in better spirits and enjoy the holidays with my family and perhaps lean upon them for a little support.

In January 2014, I redoubled my efforts to find gainful employment. I began to network with professionals in both academics and business. Things seemed to be loosening up in the job market; job fairs were popping up throughout the area. After attending one in Jackson, I was convinced that at least two of the companies represented would be interested in my services. Hope springs eternal when you are on the outside looking in.

I began to speak with people of all ages who were involved in the same process of trying to find a job and found that they were just as frustrated as I was. Many of the Millennials told me they had gone to school and worked to get good grades so that they could get a good job after graduation. Their biggest obstacle was lack of experience. I could relate to their plight and impatience. They, too, were being offered jobs paying $8-10 per hour and wondering how they could pay off their immense student loan debt on such a paltry salary.

I continued to respond to job opportunities online. As with most endeavors in life, persistence eventually pays off. I received a phone interview and was called in to take an aptitude test for a sales associate position at a local car dealership. The dealership, which had been in business for many years, recently changed hands and had a new name. After completing the aptitude test, I was invited to interview with two of the sales managers. The next day I was called in to interview with another manager. I was told they would let me know. I was encouraged. At least I had been involved in the process with actual people.

I Am Not An **Anachronism** | Don Polley

I was hired to start the following week and began a five-week training program. I was selling cars the second week I was on the lot; my training was abbreviated so that I could become a part of the sales team. I learned a great deal about the car business, car salesmen, customers and dealing with the public. This was my first involvement with computer resource management or CRM and it did not take long to realize how ineffective it could be if not kept current with up to date information. It felt good to be a useful part of an organization again and a part of an effective sales team engaged in making profit for the owner of the business.

I soon discovered the car business had a lot of turnover and that it involved working more hours than indicated during the hiring process. Not having weekends and holidays off was not conducive to the Millennial sales staff and not exactly embraced by those of us on the other end of the spectrum either. However, being a Boomer, I always made adjustments to cater to the needs of the business. I learned a lot about the interaction between Millennials and Boomers involved in the business as well as the interaction between Millennials and Boomers as car buyers.

I staggered at the amount of student loan debt that recent graduates had to assume, which had a significant impact on their car-buying decisions. I learned fairly quickly that most people who came to the lot shopping for new or used cars had already spent several hours online researching the pros and cons of their choices. It was important to try to stay as up to date on the product as possible because customers did not want to be misinformed. It seemed to me that most of the "sales pros" seemed to believe that the principles and guidelines that worked in the 20th century would be just as effective in the 21st century. Based upon my limited experience, I would disagree. The highlight of my time in the car business was the satisfaction I received after selling a car that was on the showroom floor when I was hired. I had resolved to sell it and succeeded with the help of another sales associate before I left. It seemed that 20 percent of the salespeople made 80 percent of the sales. Even with the high turnover rate I witnessed during my brief tenure, I determined that the car business was not for me.

    I had the opportunity to gain a great deal of insight and perspective from my time in the car business, but once again, as the Thanksgiving holiday approached, I was back to "virtually" trying to obtain gainful employment. I could easily understand the frustration in the world today as my generation seemed to have done a poor job of equipping and preparing the next generation for the future. Education was a good step in the right direction, but I was beginning to side with the Millennials about the return on investment over the long haul. Initially, it did not seem to be much of a bargain.

    I have always believed that you get out of education what you put into it, and I had a vested interest in its impact upon my future. I volunteered to be a mentor for Tennessee Achieves because I needed to accomplish something worthwhile and rewarding. Tennessee Achieves is a mentoring program to help high school students eligible for last dollar scholarships to handle the details of applying for college. As it turned out, the experience was not only rewarding but mutually beneficial to both the students and the mentors. I learned to appreciate some of the benefits of social media as Millennial students did not respond well to either phone calls or e-mails.

    It just did not seem fair that I was to begin yet another year unemployed. I did notice more job fairs cropping up. I could actually go and speak with human beings, which

I Am Not An **Anachronism** | Don Polley

offered me some encouragement during some difficult times. Once again, I would feel I had a firm lead on a job as I left the job fair, but then had no follow-up response or job opportunity. I continued to talk to others attending the job fairs and found myself in the same circumstance as the Millennials.

We were unwilling to accept what was offered as we felt that there would be better opportunities available down the road. Millennials had a difficult time processing being overqualified, as they had little to no job experience. We each had one thing in common; a lack of opportunity to display our potential value to a company, group or organization. As I continued along the job fair circuit, I found that the same temporary staffing services seemed to be at each one. The academic recruiters, who were at most of the larger job fairs, recommended that I pursue a master's degree, which, they said, would translate into a definitive opportunity to pursue the job of my dreams. Ironically, I had heard that story before. I had been a few years younger then and believed that my age would not be a detriment to job search.

As I continually perused the job boards online, I noticed a variety of groups, programs and individuals available online to assist in your job search activities for a fee. It occurred to me that much like in the car business, Zig Ziglar was not going to help me sell a car anymore that Dave Ramsey would assist someone in buying one off of the car lot. I continued to network, discern trends in the job market and glean the thoughts of others who were also seeking employment. I began a senior outreach program at the church I attended and became state certified to be a volunteer for the Tennessee SHIP/SMP program to assist senior citizens with open enrollment in Medicare prescription drug plans. I needed to be challenged and feel that I was making a difference in the lives of others and adding value at the same time. It was a most rewarding experience, and I recertified again in 2016.

I was also selected to be a part of a mastermind group to read and write a review for *New York Times* best-selling author Kevin Kruse, who wrote "15 Secrets Successful People Know About Time Management." When I accepted the offer, I had no idea what an impact it was going to have on my life. I had already begun the process of reassessing the direction of my life. Reviewing Kevin's book proved to be the catalyst I needed to propel my life into a different direction. As it turned out, not being able to find a job in 2015 was for me, better that getting an MBA. Once again, I resolved to turn adversity into opportunity. If there is one thing that a leader knows how to do, it is to lead.

Chapter 17
No Risk-No Reward

October 2015 turned out to be a transitional time for me in my life; I had finally found a job that would be both challenging and rewarding. I hired myself and formed my own company.

I came to this decision after attending a program hosted by John Maxwell, author of many books on leadership, including "Live 2 Lead." The event was a live cast and shown on a big screen at a local community college. Each speaker made some points that resonated with me, and I even bought Maxwell's book. He emphasized living with intentionality, and I realized that I could relate to that concept because it had been a driving force for me most of my life.

Another defining moment came during a job fair that I attended in a small town near where I lived. A coordinator with Goodwill Career Solutions offered to introduce me to a woman representing a staffing service. As the woman looked at me, she told the coordinator that she did not have time for me. That was the "slap in the face" that I needed in order to focus on what was to follow. I had grown tired of running into brick walls and determined that I could help more people if I had more freedom. As I have said before, I am the exception, not the rule. I decided that these were times that were in need of extraordinary leaders with exceptional leadership skills who were not afraid to cause a little disruption in order to succeed.

That very evening I began to brainstorm and write ideas on Post-It notes around my living room. Through the process of elimination, I decided on my top two skills after spending 35 years in the workplace: communication and problem solving. As I began my career, I experienced age discrimination in a leadership role in retail; I found myself to be

I Am Not An **Anachronism** | Don Polley

on the opposite end of the age discrimination scale as being perceived as too old at this juncture in my professional career.

I enjoyed many accomplishments and years of success as a leader over the course of my professional career and now it was time to filter that success into my two strengths. As I assessed the efforts of the past year, I decided that if I could not get a company or organization to hire me because of my age; then I would have to find a way for them to procure my services because of my age and expertise. Companies seemed to be more dependent upon empowering, supportive, and open leaders; which as it turns out was a reflection of my leadership style over my many years in business.

The challenge was to find an existing problem that I could help companies solve because of my expertise. I spent hours doing research online. I noted that employee engagement seemed to be a recurring problem and that generational diversity seemed to be the root cause of that problem. I thought hard about this; I wanted to make sure that I could resolve the issue and, at the same time, add value to any customer with whom I would do business as I intended to put my name upon my business card.

As I researched issues involved in the generational workplace, the discussions primarily revolved around Millennials and Boomers. I determined that there should be some discussion of Generation X, but for the most part it centered upon Millennials, ages 19-35, and Boomers, which would be comprised of 35 and up. My research indicated that those in senior human resources positions or hiring managers were essentially from the Boomer generation. It was completely understandable that they had difficulty relating to Millennials as they are the first generation to penetrate the workforce as tech natives.

Millennials have never known a world in which the internet did not exist, where they were not able to obtain instant answers to their questions, and did not have the capability to search online with the benefit of a search engine. I determined that the biggest cause of disconnect was in understanding. Millennials could absorb and process information so much more quickly than Boomers, many of whom had been too busy keeping up with the business to stay completely abreast of the technology. In fact, many Boomers, myself included, had resisted technology and found it to be more annoying than beneficial simply because we did not understand how to properly use it. My generation was hesitant to completely explore a device; afraid we may cause it to malfunction. Millennials were eager to get their hands on the technology and challenge it to see what it could do.

During my brainstorming phase, I also did a SWOT (strengths, weaknesses, opportunities and threats) analysis to determine what barriers I would have to overcome and assess my capability to turn any weakness into strength. I had come a long way from the smartphone that I acquired in spring 2013 while still in school. I volunteered to be a mentor for Tennessee Achieves once again in 2016 and, just like year before, my Millennial mentees had something to teach me about the benefits of social media.

This time I finally bought into social media and was on Twitter, Facebook, LinkedIn and Instagram. I resolved to turn my perceived weakness with social media into a strength. The proverbial caveman had finally come out of the cave and into the sunlight of the 21st Century. I was now familiar with Windows 7, Windows 8, Windows 10 and used an iPhone. Instead of taking a break for the holidays as I had done the past two years, I spent endless hours online researching the tremendous volume of information that was available. I continued to converse with Millennials at every opportunity to find out the biggest stumbling blocks and misconceptions they encountered once they entered into what Boomers often referred to as the "real world." I had the opportunity to be involved with Millennials when they first entered the workplace. I had gone to college with some of the best and brightest and learned a great deal about what they expected out of life.

    In January 2016 I spent several hours watching the speakers at The Peak Work Performance Summit hosted by Ron Friedman, Ph.D. I enjoyed his commentary and the insights presented by a most distinguished and renowned array of speakers. I became inspired to write a book. In today's business world, it seems, a book is the new business card. I initially got the idea from Kevin Kruse; I bounced it off some of the business professionals who lived all over the globe with whom I had communicated as a part of the Mastermind group to review Kevin's book. I always wanted to write a book, but never could seem to find the time.

    Once again I go back to Kruse and his reference to 1,440, which is the number of minutes in a day. The successful people he interviewed for his book gave me a different outlook on how to perceive time. I joined the Non-Fiction Authors Association and found a wealth of invaluable tips as I moved forward in my writing project. I give a special thanks to Stephanie Chandler for providing me the opportunity to join her group and her willingness to share her experience and expertise. I also joined Linked University to gain more insight into using social media, which is a platform that must be embraced in order to succeed in business today.

    I had to evaluate how many resources I was willing to

invest into my business venture, and this again forced me to take a hard look at my resolve and motivation. I knew from the outset that I would not be defined by the tremendous success I had enjoyed over the years. I had grown tired of running into brick walls and continually struggling to overcome obstacles introduced by upper management. Experience taught me a better way in which to get things done, and I would be able to help more people if I had more freedom to initiate my strategic plan.

My passion has always been to help others realize their potential and to open doors of opportunity to enable them to succeed. I signed a contract with a Millennial to do my marketing, and he has absolutely amazed me with his professionalism and business acumen. He designed my business card, website, and printed material in a way that I could never have accomplished on my own. He produced a video that surprisingly enabled me to be polished, genuine, and sincere.

I have gained an appreciation for members of the Millennial generation who face a variety of obstacles as they take their swing at pursuing the American dream. I marveled at the new wave of Millennial leaders, such as entrepreneur Dan Price. Price runs a successful business with integrity and stays true to his core values. He is not afraid to empower his employees as he embraces the notion that satisfying both the internal and external customer is not only be good for business, it allows it to prosper and grow. I found myself to be somewhat in awe of what Price had accomplished in initiating his successful business plan. He seemed to embrace the challenge of proving that the way business was done was becoming more and more outdated.

It reminded me of my brief stint in the car business

where they were still trying to implement 20th century techniques in order to sell cars in the 21st century. No wonder Millennials were not buying into the process; they already knew what they wanted when they walked through the door of the dealership. They just wanted someone to facilitate the sale without unnecessary pressures to change their decision. Price displayed that in business today one can be disruptive and still be customer centric and client focused. The more I learn about Millennials, the more I realize that they are not that different from me in their ideology.

    Part of the reason I chose my business model was to enable me to give back and add value to the younger generation as well as help my own generation build a bridge of understanding and engagement across the generational divide. I hope to be able to give them what we did not always receive – the best encouragement when we began our careers in the workplace many years ago. My generation made the world a better place without the benefit of Google, YouTube and mobile technology. Many times we learned things the hard way, often using brute strength and awkwardness to get the job done. Eventually we learned how to work smart as opposed to working hard, and we made more than our share of mistakes in the process.

    Millennials are going to have to be allowed to make mistakes as well, as they determine the best path for them as they head into a future that is still under construction. One thing we have in common: none of us can Google the future. Many of the jobs that Millennials starting in college today will eventually fill do not even exist yet. Boomers need to do their part to help prepare them for the unforeseen challenges that they will face.

I have resolved to pursue my passion for helping others realize their potential. I can think of no greater privilege than to work to add value to strengthen the relationships between Millennials and their older counterparts. I am not an Anachronism; I have been working my entire life to prepare me for the opportunity that lies before me, gaining value at every career stage. I find myself to be just like Millennials – a wealth of potential just waiting for the right opportunity to provide a positive impact to help mold a future of sustainable growth and continuous improvement.

Employee engagement and retention today means understanding an empowered workforce's desire for flexibility, creativity and purpose. Wisdom carries a value that goes beyond price; be grateful if you have it. Wisdom, much like experience, cannot be found on Google; it must be either gained or earned. Much like the Millennials I have interviewed over the past several months, I am excited about the opportunities that are going to come my way as we strive to leave a lasting imprint upon the future.

About the Author

Don Polley

Over 40 years of working and leading in retail, sales, and manufacturing, Don began to see the valley that exists between his generation, the Boomers, and that of the Millennials. Don began to write about this opportunity and started Don Polley and Associates to help companies bridge the gap and start to recruit, engage, and keep the very best Millennials in their workforce.

Made in the USA
Lexington, KY
03 December 2018